BUSINESS ETIQUETTE

for Students and
New Professionals

MARY CRANE

100 Things You Need to Know™
Business Etiquette
for
Students and
New Professionals

by Mary R. Crane

Copyright © 2014 Mary R. Crane

Cover design: Merryall Studio
Interior design: Diana Russell Design
Author photo: Tony Gale
Interior photos: Rod Searcey
Editorial consultant: Holly Brady

ISBN: 978-0-9890664-4-0
ebook ISBN: 978-0-9890664-5-7

Address permission requests to:
Mary Crane & Associates
New York, NY
info@marycrane.com

For more information about
Mary Crane & Associates:
www.marycrane.com

Contents

Introduction

True confession: I hate the term "etiquette."

For more than a decade, I've worked with students in leading universities and new professionals in law firms and Fortune 500 companies. Experience has taught me that, when many of my clients see or hear the word "etiquette," the small hairs on the backs of their necks begin to rise. Cringes soon follow. Too often, I know, this word conjures up an image of a little grey-haired lady, wearing safe and comfortable shoes, who criticizes the ways others sit, eat, and drink.

It's not how I like to think of myself—or of this very important subject.

As I tell my clients, if you need to prepare for this year's cotillion or next season's debutante ball, please don't retain me.

However, if you need to make a good first impression at a job interview and at the meal that often follows, let's talk. And if you wish to position yourself as a consummate professional once you enter the world of work, then I will spend as much time as you are willing to invest giving you the manners you need to navigate a variety of business-social settings.

Rather than learning hundreds of technical rules of etiquette, I'll show you how to use manners to succeed.

What's the difference between etiquette and good manners? To understand where the two diverge, it helps to know a little about the origins of the term "etiquette," something wrapped in both fact and legend.

Factually, we know the term emerged around the time of Louis XIV, the French king famously associated with converting a hunting lodge into the Palace of Versailles. According to legend, a Versailles gardener asked the king to establish a set of rules regarding who could traipse around the palace grounds and when. Louis reportedly responded by having his aides issue a daily ticket, or in French *etiquette*. Distributed to members of the royal court, each ticket included a listing of significant daily royal events and a description of appropriate attire. Over time, the daily tickets evolved to include various rules regarding correct behavior. For example, a ticket might specify how low to bow when the king approached.

Several hundred years later, Quentin Crisp, an English raconteur and writer, took issue with the exclusionary nature of the rules of etiquette. In his essay *Manners from Heaven: A Divine Guide to Good Behavior*, Crisp noted that members of the royal court who failed to follow King Louis's rules were often expelled from court. But, Crisp wrote, good manners are actually all about *inclusion*. People with good manners notice other people, address their needs, and help them feel comfortable.

An incident at another royal court, this time in nineteenth-century England, illustrates the difference between good manners and etiquette. At the end of a state dinner hosted by Queen Victoria for an African chief, guests were presented with finger bowls. Unfamiliar with finger-bowl etiquette, the chief lifted his finger bowl, raised it to his mouth, and drank the contents. I'm willing to bet that jaws dropped. Having observed the *faux pas* of her guest of honor, Queen Victoria reacted with tremendous grace. She immediately lifted her own finger bowl and drank its contents. Soon thereafter, the remaining guests followed the queen's lead. On that particular evening, every guest of Buckingham Palace consumed the contents of his or her finger bowl.

Rather than follow a rule of etiquette, the queen exhibited the best manners possible. She ensured that her guest felt comfortable and at ease.

I couldn't care less whether you know all the little rules of what I call "fish fork etiquette." Trust me on this: you can know those rules and still be the rudest person around. I do care that you acquire the very best manners possible, in part, because good manners will help you land the job, build a team, and eventually close the really big deal.

So let's put aside my aversion to certain words. Let's tackle the "100 Thing You Needs to Know" about business etiquette—and ensure you always bring your very best manners to work.

Chapter 1

Interview with Style

As a student or new professional, you will be called upon to demonstrate a working knowledge of the rules of business etiquette long before you enter the workforce.

Job interviews afford you the opportunity to demonstrate that you possess the requisite skills for a particular position. But skills are not the only thing employers seek. Employers know they can train for skills; they can't train for attitude, especially an attitude that conveys politeness.

If you want to succeed at a job interview, show a genuine interest in the prospective employer. Before the interview, research your interviewer and develop questions about the firm, company, nonprofit, or governmental entity. Demonstrate respect for a particular interviewer by arriving for your interview precisely on time and appropriately dressed. Throughout the interview, give your full attention to the prospective employer—don't even think about taking your smartphone into an interview. After the interview ends, send a handwritten thank-you note.

Good manners won't ensure that you receive a job offer. However, a display of bad manners can keep a prospective employer from appreciating the talents you've worked so hard to develop.

1. Business etiquette begins with preparation

Before every interview, do your research. Google or Bing the person or people you will meet. Make special note of any points of commonality that you uncover. If you both attended the same business school, you likely have a shared knowledge of a campus and certain professors. If you uncover that your interviewer spends part of her time as a little league coach and you're on the roster of the local softball team, make note of your shared sports interest.

As part of your research, learn everything you can about the organization and its culture. If you detect a relatively conservative culture, plan to present yourself more formally. Where the culture appears to be more relaxed, consider adopting a more informal approach.

People with good manners anticipate others' needs. Although most interviewers will have a copy of your résumé, prepare for the possibility that your information will be misplaced. Carry several additional copies of your résumé in a portfolio, keeping them neat and clean.

Your portfolio should also include a fresh pad of paper and a pen. Feel free to take notes throughout any interview. Jot down a word or two that helps you remember important questions. However, keep in mind that this is a job interview and not a class lecture. Don't get so caught up in taking notes that you fail to make eye contact with your interviewer or engage in a genuine conversation.

2. Dress for the job you hope to land

Your research should help you identify appropriate attire for the interview, which will vary from industry to industry and culture to culture. In selecting your interview outfit, choose attire that helps position you as a successful member of a particular industry or profession. In other words, you should fake it 'til you make it.

Law students interviewing for a position with a very conservative law firm obviously should interview in conservative attire, including suits and ties for the gentlemen and business suits for the ladies. (Ladies, in some parts of the country, this still means a suit comprised of a skirt or dress and a jacket.) In contrast, business students interviewing with an Internet startup may find that more relaxed attire is the norm.

Before you head to an interview, pay particular attention to your hair. Ensure that it's neatly styled and that no stray hairs will fall into your face during the course of the interview.

Finally, select your interview shoes carefully. Like the rest of your outfit, what's appropriate varies by industry. For a more conservative employer, gentlemen should consider dark, lace-up shoes, and ladies should plan on closed-toe pumps. In all cases, confirm your shoes are shined and the heels are not worn down.

3. Arrive on time and alone

Showing up precisely on time may be the easiest part of any job interview. And yet, prospective candidates frequently arrive late. When they do so, they demonstrate a complete lack of respect for an interviewer's time.

Arrive early for every interview. If you need to kill some time, walk around the block or grab a quick coffee or tea. Give yourself plenty of time to pass through any security that might be present in a particular office building. Greet every staff member you encounter with eye contact, a smile, and a warm hello.

You will likely be directed to take a seat in the reception area. Feel free to do so. However, some research indicates that if you remain standing in a confident manner—think the Jolly Green Giant stance—cortisol will decrease and testosterone will increase in your body, helping you feel more confident. Before an interview, take advantage of every confidence-building technique you can.

Attend interviews on your own. With increasing frequency employers tell me about job candidates who ask whether a parent may accompany them to an interview. If you have a "helicopter parent," by all means, immediately impose a ground stop upon him or her. Take charge of your own future.

4. Give every interviewer your full attention

An interview gives you the opportunity to establish a relationship with a prospective employer. Demonstrate your interest in an interviewer by giving him or her your complete, undivided attention.

In one recent survey, 30 percent of prospective employers complained that applicants checked their smartphones or texted during the course of an interview. Avoid this mistake. If you absolutely must carry a smartphone or any other electronic gadget, turn it off—not to vibrate, not to blink, completely off—before the interview begins. Or if you can, avoid taking your gadgets to an interview by storing them in a school locker or leaving them in your car.

Caveat: If you expect a genuine emergency phone call— for example, if your spouse is due to go into labor at any moment—explain the potential emergency interruption to your interviewer at the very beginning of your meeting, and turn your smartphone to vibrate.

5. Greet every interviewer professionally

Every time you meet an interviewer, stand, make eye contact, and smile. State your name clearly. Extend your right hand for a handshake, holding your hand perfectly perpendicular to the ground. (If you allow your hand to dip over to a 45-degree angle, you're more likely to deliver a limp-wrist, cold-fish handshake—something you definitely want to avoid.)

Firmly grasp the other person's hand, pump once or twice, and then release.

If you have an unusual or a difficult-to-pronounce name, make sure that you slow your speech and clearly artic-ulate your name. In fact, you may wish to help others pronounce your name by providing them with a clue. For example, someone named Vaux might say, "It's pronounced *Vaux*, like *faux* in *faux fur* or *faux leather.*"

In the United States, if you and your interviewer are close in age, feel free to address your interviewer using his or her first name. However, if your interviewer appears to be much older than you, an organizational leader (CEO, managing partner), or from another country, use the more formal social title of "Mr." or "Ms."

As soon as someone asks you to use his or her first name, by all means, do.

6. Listen, respond, ask

Throughout the interview, listen carefully to each question you receive. Take just a moment to formulate your thoughts. Then deliver your response in a polite manner.

Certain questions are out of bounds, including questions unrelated to the job for which an employer is hiring. Questions about race, sex, national origin, birthplace, age, disability, and marital or family status are illegal. Should you receive a question about one of these topics, try to gracefully redirect the conversation. Alternatively, consider answering the "intent" of the question. If someone asks whether you are a United States citizen—a question that is permissible—you might reply, "I'm authorized to work in the United States."

Inevitably, you will receive a question that will be perfectly legal but one that you weren't prepared to answer. Answer as well as you can. One job candidate recently told me she was surprised when asked, "What's the one question I should ask you but haven't?" My recommended response: "Are you available to start on Monday?"

No matter what question you receive, do not lie. If you land the job and if your employer learns of your misrepresentation, in some states, you can be fired without recourse.

Do carry some questions to an interview. Employers tell me they immediately eliminate from consideration any job candidate who does not ask questions. In their minds, a lack of questions indicates a lack of genuine interest in the position. Obviously, these questions should *not* include inquiries like: *How soon can I take my first vacation? When can I expect my first raise? If I don't use all of my sick days, will I lose them?*

7. Know table manners

Many prospective employers invite job candidates to an interview meal. Remember this meal is a continuation of the interview. Even if the temperature outside hovers around 110 degrees in the shade, keep your suit coat or jacket on if your interviewer continues to wear her jacket. And while the conversation you encounter may be slightly more relaxed than the formal interview, you must continue to speak in a business-appropriate manner.

We'll cover business dining more thoroughly in Chapter 4. For now understand that you should choose menu options that you know how to eat—an interview meal is not the time for experimentation—and that you can eat neatly. When you initially scan the menu, avoid the least and most expensive options. In terms of the number of courses you should order, mirror your host or hostess. If he or she orders both an appetizer and an entrée, no matter what your hunger level is, you should do the same.

Employers tell me they schedule interview meals in part to observe how a job candidate interacts with waitstaff. They believe that the job candidate who acts dismissively toward the waitstaff will likely act in a similar manner with office support staff. You will never err by saying "please" and "thank you" to the people who serve you.

8. Conquer callback interview receptions

Some organizations invite groups of job candidates to extensive callback interviews. These often occur over multiple days, generally a Friday and Saturday, and may include a social component. The latter affords employers the opportunity to see how prospective job candidates perform outside the formal interview setting.

As a job candidate, prepare for the social event in the same manner as you prepare for the interviews. Contact the recruiting team and request a list of potential guests. Research every guest, looking for shared history and common interests. Prepare some questions that you can ask any other attendee. For example: *What do you like most about working at the firm? How long have you been employed by the company? What's the most exciting project you've tackled?*

Prior to attending the reception, eat a small snack. This will help ensure you don't arrive feeling half-starved, always a possibility after a long day of interviews.

When you arrive, request a beverage and hold it in your left hand, keeping your right hand available for hand-shakes. Then, immediately start to "work" the room. Introduce yourself to other guests and engage in interesting conversations.

9. Limit alcohol consumption

I talk to enough students and new professionals to know that what they should drink and how much they may drink at interview meals and callback receptions top their lists of questions and quandaries.

Everyone knows not to drink too much. Becoming tipsy in front of a prospective employer is a bad idea. The concern my clients more frequently raise is this: Should I try to keep up with my host? If they move on to a third and fourth cocktail or glass of wine, won't I look like a wet blanket if I don't join in?

Here's what I recommend:

- At a post-interview lunch, skip alcohol altogether. Stick with fruit juice, soda, iced tea, or water as your beverage of choice.

- At a post-interview dinner, skip high-octane cocktails, which may affect your good judgment. If you choose to drink, nurse one glass of wine throughout the entire meal.

- At a callback reception, don't lose your focus. I'd prefer that you stick with fruit juice, soda, and water. However, if you decide on a glass of wine, be sure to nurse it throughout the event.

- If you don't drink alcoholic beverages, don't feel pressured to do so.

When someone encourages you to enjoy a second or third glass of wine, simply state, "Thanks very much for the offer. I still have (*some studying to tackle* or *emails to return* or *a project I need to address*) later tonight. I need to make sure I stay focused." If the pressure continues, allow waitstaff to refill your wine glass, and just don't take another sip.

10. Express your thanks

You know you should express your appreciation for an interview. Email allows you to express gratitude quickly, while a handwritten note makes your expression more memorable—especially in a world where many professionals receive hundreds of emails daily.

Email or snail mail, which is better? Try both. The day of your interview, send an email to everyone with whom you met that begins: "I'll send a more appropriate thank you via mail, but I wanted to immediately express my appreciation for your time today." Then remark on something you discussed in the interview.

Within 48 hours, follow up with a handwritten thank-you note. That note should look something like this:

Dear (name of interviewer):

Thank you for making time in your schedule to meet with me.

State one thing about the interview that made it memorable.

Describe your follow-up.

Sincerely,

So after an interview, Adriana Nunez might draft a post-interview thank-you note that looks something like this:

Dear Michelle,

Thank you for making time in your schedule to meet with me. I appreciated learning about the exciting prospects for analytics professionals at Cloudera. Next week, I'll follow up with the company's recruiting department to discern our next steps.

Sincerely,

Adriana Nunez

Unless you know that texting is an interviewer's preferred method of communication, please never text your thanks for an interview. Should you disregard this advice, avoid any texting abbreviations or unusual spellings that the recipient may not understand.

Chapter 2

Support Your Boss

With a few notable exceptions, today's students and new professionals encounter relatively flat work hierarchies, especially when compared to the ones that existed just a generation or two ago. Nonetheless, distinctions remain between bosses and workers. Your boss maintains the ultimate decision making authority when it comes to hiring, firing, and assigning tasks. As a new professional, you will be charged with accomplishing tasks. Always remember, as a new professional your top priority at work is to help your boss accomplish his or her goals.

Everything you do in the workplace should make your boss and direct supervisor look good. That means you should *always* act in a respectful manner no matter who you interact with or when. Dress in business-appropriate attire. Speak appropriately, which sometimes means not saying anything at all. Keep client secrets, and do not speak behind your boss's back.

Inevitably you will encounter the "less than perfect" boss. When this occurs, manage conflicts with tact. Should you decide to seek other job opportunities, never burn a bridge.

11. Remember, your boss is your boss

As organizations have flattened, the separation between bosses and their employees has diminished. However, the distinction remains. A boss occupies a uniquely powerful and responsible position.

When confronted with an especially open and supportive boss, too many students and new professionals forget this critical distinction. So let's make this clear: your boss is your boss. No matter how supportive he or she may be, your boss is not your best friend. Nor is he or she a substitute Mom or Dad. Every boss should be treated with respect, even when you disagree with him or her.

Your boss owes you certain duties and obligations. First and foremost, he or she must ensure the safety of your work environment. You should be able to arrive at work on a day-to-day basis without fear of being harmed by equipment or other employees. In addition, every employer has a responsibility to provide fair compensation for work performed correctly.

Beyond these duties, the best bosses provide employees with challenging work projects. They give loads of feedback. Some even manage to inspire their workers to achieve.

12. You owe your boss certain duties

Just as every boss owes certain duties to his or her employee, every new or established professional owes certain duties to his or her boss. Employees with good manners do the following:

■ **Ensure that the boss always looks good.**
This means: no surprises. Keep your boss informed of the status of projects, especially delays and significant problems that you encounter. Turn in projects that are "client ready," i.e., free of typos and stains or stray markings. If you become aware of some office or client communication that could affect your boss, make your boss aware of it.

■ **Demonstrate loyalty.**
Inevitably your boss will make a decision with which you disagree. Unless that decision is illegal or immoral, you have an obligation to support your boss. Do not disagree or criticize your boss publicly, especially among your peers. Should you choose to share your disagreement with your boss, do so behind closed doors (see #19).

■ **Show respect.**
There are certain people who deserve your respect simply because of the position they occupy. For example, when a judge makes a decision, we may disagree with the conclusions he or she reached. Nonetheless, we respect the authority of the courts. Every boss occupies a position that in and of itself deserves respect.

■ **Express appreciation.**
Your boss has given you an opportunity to prove your capabilities. Show some appreciation. A genuine "thank you" can help build a long-term, mutually beneficial working relationship.

13. Dress with respect

When you enter the world of work, the attire you wear to the office creates an impression that extends to your boss. Always dress in a manner that reflects well upon both of you. Your attire should also demonstrate respect for any clients with whom you'll interact.

If you have opted to work for a more conservative organization—say, a white-shoe law firm or a state legislature—you should dress in a more conservative manner which likely means suits for both men and women. If you have taken a job in a fashion-forward organization, you should dress in a manner that communicates your understanding and appreciation of fashion.

At a very minimum, you should:

- avoid dirty, stained, torn, or frayed clothing;
- avoid clothing bearing words or images that others might find offensive;
- avoid clothing that reveals cleavage, excessive chest hair, whale tails, and plumbers cracks.

Always wear business-appropriate shoes to work. If your commute involves a long walk or bike ride, feel free to wear more comfortable shoes while you're in transit. Before you enter your workplace, change shoes.

14. Act professionally

Everything you do in conjunction with work should communicate your respect for internal and external clients.

Before you walk into an office building, remove your ear buds. Acknowledge other people you know in the building lobby. Whenever you board an elevator, recognize any coworkers you encounter. As you walk to or from your workstation or office, greet others you meet along the way. First thing in the morning, check in with your boss. Do another check-in at the end of your workday.

Be punctual to all meetings. This demonstrates your respect for others' time. Know your boss's expectations regarding smartphone use during meetings. If he or she expects your complete attention, before any meeting begins, turn your smartphone off.

Listen to office gossip; however, never repeat it. Gossip tends to contain some nugget of truth and a lot of embellishment or conjecture. To ensure you don't repeat a false or inaccurate statement and become known as a purveyor of untruths, never repeat gossip.

Understand the chain of command. When you disagree with a coworker, work with your coworker to develop a solution. When you disagree with your boss, address him or her directly. Never elevate a matter to someone's supervisor without his or her knowledge.

15. Complete projects on time

Tackle every assignment you receive in a timely manner.

Should you experience unexpected delays or interruptions, do not withhold this information from your supervisor until the very last moment. Remember, no surprises. Inform your boss as quickly as possible. This allows your boss to adequately manage the expectations of his or her own internal and external clients.

Inevitably, you will require a coworker's input to complete a project. Should your coworker fail to perform in a timely manner, in most cases you'll remain responsible. Telling a boss *I emailed Jim in marketing for his input, but he hasn't gotten back to me* won't cut it. Find ways to work with others and to complete projects on time.

If you report to multiple bosses and their competing demands make it difficult for you to complete any one project, work with your bosses to prioritize your assignments.

16. Always interact professionally with clients and customers

Clients and customers are the lifeblood of every organization. Without them, you don't have a job. Always ensure customers and clients feel treasured like the valued people they are.

Whenever a client or customer is present, give that person one hundred percent of your attention. End all personal conversations, phone calls, emailing, texting, and the like.

To demonstrate your respect, when you first meet a client or customer, use the social titles of "Mr." or "Ms." Do this whether your first interaction involves a face-to-face meeting or an email. Once the client or customer requests that you use a first name, by all means do.

Anticipate a client or customer's needs. When a client arrives at your offices for an extended visit, direct her to a private office if possible where she can address any other business needs she might have. Offer her a beverage. Make sure she knows where restrooms are located.

Protect client confidences. Every client must know that whatever he or she says to you or to your boss will not be repeated outside the confines of the professional relationship. Employees who violate client confidences break every rule of business etiquette. They also risk violating various rules of professional conduct and may be found in violation of the law.

17. Manage introductions

You may be called upon to introduce clients, customers, guests, and fellow employees to coworkers, including your boss. In general, here's the rule: state the most important person's name first. Then, introduce the less important person to the person who is more important.

So, you should introduce:

- a younger person to an older person;
- a junior employee to a senior employee or executive;
- a coworker to a peer from another company;
- a coworker to a customer or client;
- a spouse, partner, or significant other to a supervisor or boss.

Let's try one. As a junior associate at a law firm, you need to introduce a client (Michelle Perez) to the head of the firm's Mergers & Acquisitions practice group (Simon Stephens). You might say, "Ms. Perez, I'd like you to meet the head of our M&A group, Simon Stephens. Simon, this is Ms. Michelle Perez. She's the general counsel at Quicken Loans. Genevieve Tucker in Tax has been her key point of contact with the firm."

18. Request feedback

Organizations have become increasingly aware of the importance of providing feedback to junior employees. Nonetheless, your boss's day-to-day workload may prevent him or her from scheduling regular meetings to update you on your progress. When this happens, successful new professionals take charge of their careers.

- **Schedule a regular meeting.**
  Politely explain your need to receive regular feedback in order to improve your performance. You might say, "I understand I need to develop in this position, and I value your input. May we schedule a regular meeting to discuss my performance?"

- **Welcome any feedback you receive.**
  Few bosses will take the time to provide in-depth feedback unless they genuinely wish to see an employee grow and develop. Listen to any feedback you receive—especially the feedback that is less than positive—and learn from it.

- **React.**
  When a boss points out an area in which you can improve your performance, demonstrate that you value this feedback by reacting appropriately. If this means you need to change a behavior, change.

- **File positive feedback.**
  Keep an electronic or paper file of every bit of positive feedback that you receive. When you experience a bad day at work—and you will—a quick scan of this file can be an absolute lifesaver. It can also help you identify your strengths.

19. Work with a difficult boss

At some point in your career you will undoubtedly encounter a "less than perfect" boss. You may even encounter an abusive boss—one who engages in verbal abuse, threats, intimidation, or humiliation; or one who sabotages work performance. Here's a sad fact: according to one survey, 15 percent of employees say they have witnessed bullying at work, and approximately 72 percent of the time, the bully is the boss.

No worker should be abused. If you feel intimidated or humiliated, report your concerns to Human Resources. If your concerns are not addressed, consider looking for other employment.

If, however, your boss is merely "difficult," there may be reason to tough it out. Before you jump ship, carefully consider whether a year or two of stressful and difficult work may be worth the experience or knowledge you will acquire. Lots of successful professionals attribute their long-term career advancement to a particularly difficult boss with whom they worked in the early stages of their career.

Should you decide to work with a difficult boss, be prepared to set limits. Point out when you believe your boss has crossed a line. Express your concerns or complaints using "I" statements. At the end of a polite confrontation, thank your boss for his or her time and get back to work.

A conversation might go like this: "Excuse me, Steve. Can I have a minute of your time? I understand your concerns with our pricing proposal, and it wasn't helpful that you raised them in front of the junior analysts. I'd appreciate it if you could raise concerns like this in private. Thanks."

20. When you decide to move on

According to a recent study conducted by the US Department of Labor, the average 25-year-old will have worked 6.3 jobs between the ages of 18 and 25. DeVry University's Career Advisory Board projects those employees will work a total of 12 to 15 different jobs over the course of their lifetime.

When it's time for you to move on, always behave with tact and grace. With regards to your boss or supervisor, communicate your decision to move on in a face-to-face meeting. Inquire how you can assist with transitioning work to a replacement. Avoid using an email blast to announce your departure. Rather, share your decision with coworkers in private conversations. Decide how you will use social networking sites to stay in touch with work colleagues who have become members of your professional or personal networks.

Set aside some time to learn from your employment experience. What new skills did you acquire? What did you learn about yourself, your natural aptitudes, and areas where you can improve your performance?

As you leave, never burn a bridge. In the course of a lifetime, you will be amazed at the people who will float in and out of your life. The coworker or boss you leave behind today may reemerge as a valued client or customer in the future. Work to maintain relationships.

Chapter 3

Work with Colleagues

If your first priority at work is to make sure the boss looks good, your second priority is to build effective relationships with coworkers. In today's world of work—one in which we are truly interdependent—these relationships can be absolutely critical. Your success or failure will be determined in part by how well you work with others.

Of all the "people challenges" faced by students and new professionals, the one that leaves them feeling most flummoxed is the challenge of working with administrative staff—especially staff who possess more day-to-day practical and institutional knowledge than they have. No doubt about it, when you're brand new, supervising someone who is both established and entrenched can be difficult. However, if you succeed in this capacity, you will build relationships that can propel your career forward.

Working with others inevitably results in disagreements. No two people see eye to eye all the time. Professionals who possess a fundamental understanding of business etiquette respectfully manage their disagreements with others.

21. Work as a team player

As a student, much of your success was determined by how well you performed on individual projects. You either scored well on a test or you didn't. As a new professional you will find that you are often assigned to team projects. As such, your success will be measured by how well the entire group performs.

Understand your role. Have you been tasked with leading the group? Then you are responsible for developing an overall game plan, assigning specific tasks to individual team members, coordinating the effort, and driving the project to completion in a timely manner. Have you been assigned to a supporting role on a team? Then you must complete each specific task that has been assigned to you within the requisite time frame. Additionally, you must be prepared to assist other team members when your help is needed.

Always act in a respectful and supportive manner. When others suggest a method for tackling a particular issue, hear them out. When others ask for your input, jump at the opportunity to contribute. When someone fails to perform or produces a contribution that others view as substandard, assume the role of problem solver. Rather than laying blame, pointing fingers, or saying "that's not my problem," develop solutions that ensure the final project is delivered on time.

22. Show respect and empathy for others

People with good manners demonstrate their respect for other people in a myriad of ways, from acknowledging another's presence with a simple "hello" or "good morning" to ensuring that the language they use never offends. People with good manners also show empathy for others. When they ask a coworker to stay late to complete a project, they acknowledge the impact of their request on that coworker's personal life.

Look for opportunities to show your respect and empathy for others:

- Pull yourself out of your own little world and acknowledge every person you encounter, from the least experienced intern to the company CEO.

- Avoid interrupting others when they speak.

- Understand and respect another's need to focus on projects. Don't drop by his or her office or workstation for unnecessary conversations.

- Because every email represents an interruption, avoid unnecessary emails or texts.

- When you see someone struggling with an armload of paper or electronic gadgets, offer to assist.

- Never leave a copy machine empty—for heaven's sake, add paper to any empty paper tray—and never leave an empty coffeepot on a heated burner.

23. Work effectively with support staff

At the earliest stages of your career, many members of the support staff will know more about the day-to-day requirements of your job than you do. You'll catch up soon enough. For now, it's important that you understand these staff members can make or break you. Give them lots of reasons to want to help you succeed.

Earlier we addressed the responsibilities your boss owes to you as well as the ones you owe to your boss (see #11 and #12). You owe certain responsibilities to the members of the support staff with whom you regularly work, including the following:

- **Communication** – Maintain two-way communication with staff members. Ask for their input. Ensure that you share all relevant information, especially information they need to complete tasks.

- **Feedback** – Give regular feedback. Provide recognition for jobs well done. Offer constructive criticism when required.

- **Autonomy** – Give staff members as much autonomy as they are able to manage well. Interfere only when necessary.

- **Facilitate work** – Ensure that staff members have all the information and tools they need to complete an assigned task. Be available to answer questions and provide guidance.

- **Recognize and respect that staff have lives outside of work** – Finally, keep relationships with staff members professional. Remember, your boss is neither your best friend nor a substitute Mom or Dad. Support staff members shouldn't play these roles either. Don't "friend" members of the support team on Facebook. Keep focused on the work you need to do and how you can most effectively accomplish tasks together.

24. Navigate open floor plans

In many offices, staff members are seated in open floor plans, where private conversations are nearly impossible. To the extent that you supervise staff assigned to cubicles, demonstrate a respect for their space. Do not barge into a cubicle, immediately take a seat, and begin to assign work. Instead, approach a cubicle barrier as if it were a wall, knock, and ask if the person has a moment to talk.

If you've been assigned to a cubicle, always be conscious of your coworkers and their need to focus on tackling tasks. Avoid disruptive behaviors. Should you need to have a conversation with someone located in another cubicle, please do not stand and shout over the cubicle partitions. Rather, walk to the other cubicle and conduct a quiet, private conversation. Similarly, when placing phone calls, lower your voice, and please avoid any private phone call that might disturb or disrupt others.

Be conscious of the impact your lunch or snack choices could have on fellow cubicle workers. Avoid loud, crunchy foods as well as foods with strong odors.

If the nature of your work requires that you constantly float from one workstation to another, leave each workstation you occupy as neat and as tidy as you found it when you arrived.

25. Request and offer help

You already know that "please" and "thank you" are magical words that can facilitate working relationships. If you are not accustomed to using these words, when you enter the world of work, start using them immediately. Being polite requires little additional effort on your part, and it pays off in dividends.

By the way, people really do like seeing and hearing the words "thank you" over abbreviations like "thx." More than one senior professional has told me that, if someone can't bother to write "thanks," he should skip it altogether.

When you request assistance from a coworker, avoid apologizing for your request. Some studies indicate that women professionals, in particular, tend to pepper their language with apologies. There's no need for you to apologize to a coworker when you ask her to perform a task that falls within her job description. However, watch the tone of your requests. You're likely not in a position to issue orders. And even if you are, keep in mind that you need your coworkers to help you succeed. No one likes to be ordered around.

When you see others in need of help and you are fully capable of helping, by all means offer your assistance. Doing so increases the odds that you will be viewed as a team player. However, remember, you have offered *assistance*. You have not offered to take ownership of the project or to lead it.

26. Work as an effective team member

When assigned to a team project—and new professionals are increasingly assigned to team projects—you owe certain duties to each member of your team. These include the following:

■ **Communicate.**
Share all information relevant to the completion of a project. When in doubt, more sharing beats less. Avoid becoming known as the one team member who failed to share a critical piece of data.

■ **Use skills wisely.**
Take advantage of each team member's unique skill sets. Encourage "big idea" people to brainstorm and encourage "detail" people to create standard operating procedures for the team.

■ **Provide feedback.**
Recognize others for their hard work. Say positive things about the team publicly. Give constructive feedback privately.

■ **Plan.**
Think through your actions and the impact they will have on other team members. Understand and be sensitive to potential competing work demands.

■ **Be available.**
Avoid wasting the valuable time of other team members. If the team has been called upon to work in close physical proximity, let others know before you step away. If the team is scattered around the globe, let others know when you will be reachable electronically.

27. Hear—*but do not repeat*— office gossip

I've yet to encounter an office that has managed to free itself from gossip. In fact, one research team from the University of Amsterdam found that 90 percent of all office conversation qualifies as gossip, while researchers at the Georgia Institute of Technology concluded that gossip made up 15 percent of office email—a percentage that seems low to me.

It turns out that lots of employees use gossip as a means of connecting with coworkers. However, repeating gossip can negatively impact a workplace. Gossip builds distrust, and when coworkers don't trust each other, team projects suffer. When work product suffers, the best employees start looking for other places to work.

You will likely encounter two types of office gossip: 1) gossip pertaining to a coworker, which generally calls into question that person's character or ability; or 2) gossip pertaining to the organization as a whole, which often involves a change that's about to or may need to happen. In both cases, the gossip likely contains rumor and speculation. It *may* contain some nugget of truth.

Because you can learn a nugget of truth, I won't suggest that you disregard every bit of office gossip that you hear. However, because it may be impossible to discern the true from false nuggets, never repeat gossip. Also be aware that you could be held legally liable for repeating any gossip that rises to the level of "malicious harassment."

28. Handle differences of opinion tactfully

In the course of your work, disagreements will arise. You must manage those differences with tact on your own—without elevating issues to your boss. Doing so not only demonstrates that you have good manners, it also demonstrates that you are a professional who can manage all of the exigencies of the day-to-day workplace.

Whenever you need to resolve a difference of opinion or a conflict, consider the following three-step process:

- **Step 1 – Acknowledgment.** Too often, people ignore or avoid conflict, hoping that somehow it will miraculously disappear. Resolving conflict requires an acknowledgment of its existence.

- **Step 2 – Understanding.** Parties to a disagreement or conflict must develop a shared understanding of the underlying facts and their impact. This requires an understanding of the filters (our underlying assumptions and beliefs) through which each of us views and understands a particular problem or situation.

- **Step 3 – Agreement.** Parties should jointly develop an agreement for moving forward.

Caveat: If someone says or does something that you believe to be a threat to your safety, don't try to resolve the situation yourself. Immediately meet with your supervisor and a representative of the organization's human resources department.

29. Know what to say

Over the course of your professional life, you will spend more of your waking hours with coworkers and colleagues than you will with many of the other important people who inhabit your world—including spouses, partners, and significant others. Doing so requires lots of forbearance. Build and maintain relationships that are professional, yet pleasant. Avoid becoming too involved in others' personal lives.

However, some significant events in a coworker's personal life may warrant your acknowledgment. In such cases, here are some things you may consider saying:

For an engagement or wedding – *Congratulations! I wish you all the best!*

For a pregnancy – *Congratulations!* (And that's it. Please do not ask: *Was it planned? Do you want the baby? Are you coming back to work?* And unless you explicitly receive her permission, never touch a pregnant woman's abdomen. In fact, with the exception of handshakes, avoid any sort of touching in the office that could be misconstrued.)

For a miscarriage – *I'm sorry for your loss.*

For a divorce – *I'm sorry.*

For an illness – *All of us here are pulling for you and sending positive energy your way.*

When someone dies – *I'm sorry for your loss.*

30. Seek out newcomers

As a new professional, make a commitment to meet your coworkers and colleagues as quickly as possible. In many cases, you'll want to build professional relationships that will further your career. Actively seek out mentors and sponsors, senior professionals who will give you challenging assignments that allow you to shine.

At the same time, constantly make an effort to meet new people who join your company, firm, or organization. Lateral hires can help you expand your thinking about a particular industry. They can also expose you to new and different ways of approaching work or a particular problem.

As you move on, reach out to newcomers who are just beginning their first forays into the world of work. Learn about their interests, including what they hope to accomplish professionally. Seek to develop newcomers. Identify their existing skills and look for opportunities to help them grow. Once they develop the ability and capacity to handle certain projects, off-load some of your work to them. Doing so will allow them to develop new competencies while you focus on your career.

Chapter 4

Master Business Meals

Once you enter the world of work, you will receive invitations to numerous business-social events, including business meals. You may find that you frequently dine with your boss and coworkers in neighborhood restaurants and bistros. If you're lucky, you'll be invited to business meals hosted in some of the world's finest restaurants. When you're invited to a business meal, make sure that you take your best manners with you.

We've already discussed that people with good manners look for ways to help others feel comfortable. Keep this in mind when making key business meal decisions. If your boss prefers to eat his or her meals on the run, avoid scheduling lunches with your boss at a high-end restaurant known for its slow service. Similarly, when deciding what to eat, take your cues from your host. If the person with whom you are dining has decided to forgo an appetizer and simply orders an entrée, you should do the same.

If you are not already comfortable with navigating a place setting, get comfortable today. And by all means, learn how to work with restaurant waitstaff. When you're uncertain what to do, these professionals can positively save you.

31. Select the "right" restaurant

Once you enter the world of work, seek out three different styles of restaurants and become a regular at each:

■ A relatively inexpensive restaurant, such as a neighborhood diner or bar. Be aware that some of your most valued colleagues and clients will prefer quick meals at a neighborhood "joint" over lengthy repasts in an elegant dining room filled with fancy linens and exotic floral arrangements. No less than gazillionaire Warren Buffet prefers root beer floats at family-owned Piccolo Pete's over any of Omaha's swankier dining establishments.

■ A mid-priced restaurant, one to which you would feel comfortable taking your boss or an important client; and

■ A high-end, fancy restaurant. Save this location for those very special meals you want to share with others to celebrate the accomplishment of significant goals.

As you consider the specific restaurants where you wish to become a regular, be cognizant of the food options they offer. Make sure the restaurants you choose can accommodate colleagues who are vegetarians or have other dietary restrictions.

32. Arrive on time and be seated

Although some business meals will be more social in nature, all of them remain business events. Just as you should arrive on time for every meeting to which you are invited—it's one of the ways professionals demonstrate their respect for one another's time—you should arrive on time for every business meal you attend. This is especially important if you are a junior member of the staff dining with someone who is more senior, or a client or customer.

If you host a business meal and if the restaurant takes reservations, by all means, make them. This will ensure you and your guests are seated at your preferred dining time.

When you arrive at a restaurant, check in with any maître d' or hostess. In some restaurants, a maître d' will not seat individual guests until the entire party arrives. When you encounter this, move to the side of the maître d's station so that other parties can be seated. Then, as soon as your entire party arrives, reconnect with the maître d'. If a hostess offers to seat individual guests as they arrive, by all means be seated.

If you and a guest arrive at a restaurant together, you may find yourself following the maître d' to a table, at which point he may pull out a dining chair. This situation is a little tricky. Technically, regardless of the diners' genders, the most important guest should be seated in this chair. So when a female senior partner in a Wall Street law firm shares lunch with a male client and the maître d' pulls out a chair, the male client should immediately be seated.

However, in some parts of the country—and here I'm thinking about my clients in the Deep South—many gentlemen say they would feel uncomfortable taking a seat before a lady, even if the hostess is the toughest litigator in the jurisdiction. In this case, a hostess has two options: she may put her client at ease by taking the seat or she may say to the client, "Please, today you're a guest of the firm," and offer the seat to her client. The second approach carries with it one additional advantage: if waitstaff has heard this remark, they now know who is hosting the table. At the end of the meal, the check should be delivered automatically to the hostess.

33. Make your menu selection

Soon after you are seated, the host or hostess or some member of the waitstaff will present you with a menu. Quickly review your options keeping the following in mind:

- No matter what your hunger level may be, initially plan on ordering two courses. If you are a particularly light eater, consider ordering two appetizers instead of an appetizer and an entrée. When you place your order, match the number of courses you order with that of the other diners. If everyone else skips the appetizer, you should do the same.

- Avoid the most and least expensive items on the menu.

- Avoid any item you don't know how to eat as well as any item that might be messy to eat. As far as I'm concerned, nothing beats a juicy burger on a toasted bun. However, because of the mess it makes of my hands, I never order a burger at a business lunch. The same rule applies to pasta with red sauce, especially if I've worn a white suit. I view an order of *pasta fra diavolo* as an invitation to disaster.

- Avoid any food items that may trigger an allergy. No one wants to see you become ill. And everyone wants to accommodate any religious dietary restrictions you may follow. However, please avoid asking a kitchen to jump through hoops to accommodate any quirky food preferences you might have.

34. Time business discussions

Use the time between when you and your fellow diners are seated and when you place your food order to connect with others socially. Never underestimate the importance of this time. The strongest business relationships are built upon a foundation of mutual trust that develops when people genuinely know each other.

Once the table's food order has been placed, the most senior person at the table or the host may take the lead and raise a business matter. This can be as simple as stating, "Hey, let's just take a few moments to talk about the progress we've made in our web marketing algorithm development," or "Let's update you quickly on the status of the case." If you are the most junior member at the dining table, your contributions to these conversations should always show respect for other participants.

If you are the most junior member and wish to raise a work-related topic, but others appear averse to a business conversation, temporarily put the topic on a back burner.

Caveat: In some private clubs, business discussions are prohibited. Adhere to the rules of the club and use discussions at these locations to deepen and enhance personal relationships.

35. Navigate the table setting

Don't let a fancy table setting confuse you. Navigating it is relatively easy as long as you remember to keep other diners and the waitstaff in mind.

Don't place anything on the tabletop—including your keys, sunglasses, or smartphone.

Ladies, place your handbag in your lap. If it's too large for your lap, place it on the floor near your feet. Please do not hang it off your chair, where it may be knocked off; or on the floor near the back of your chair, where other diners or the waitstaff might trip over it. Gentlemen, if you've carried a computer bag to the restaurant, stash it near your feet or in the restaurant's cloakroom.

As soon as you are seated, place your napkin in your lap. Please do not unfurl your napkin flamboyantly as if to make the sign of Zorro. Rather, discretely unfold it in half and place it on your lap. Your napkin should remain in your lap throughout the course of the meal. Use it to briefly dab your lips before you drink a beverage. Should you need to excuse yourself from the table, place your napkin in your chair. Return your napkin to the tabletop at the end of a meal.

Use silverware starting from the outside of the place setting and working in. Once you use a piece of silverware, never return it to the tabletop. (See #36 for a tip on where to rest silverware to communicate to the waitstaff that you have completed a particular course.)

A few other things to keep in mind regarding managing business meals:

If you are seated closest to some item that may be passed (a basket of rolls, a plate of butter, salad dressing, salt and pepper, cream, a plate of lemon slices for iced tea, etc.), keep in mind that your fellow diners may want what you have. Lift the basket of rolls and offer it to a fellow diner, remembering that you should always offer before you take.

Technically, anything passed should move counterclockwise around a table. Quite frankly, I couldn't care less whether you pass clockwise or counterclockwise as long as all passed items move in the same direction.

If an item is passed to you—for example, a basket of rolls—and you demure because you are watching your carb intake, please don't place the item back on the table. Continue to pass the item until it's clear that everyone has had the opportunity to take what they would like.

36. Hold silverware correctly

There *is* a right way and a wrong way to hold your silverware. If you fail to know this, will you miss out on a job offer? Will you fail to close the deal? Probably not. But just as you should know how to tie a shoelace and download an app, you ought to know how to correctly hold and manage silverware.

In the United States and a few countries in South America, diners generally use what is called the "zigzag" or "American" style. Begin with your fork in your left hand, tines pointed down, and knife in your right hand. Cut two to three bite-sized pieces of food. Then, put your knife down, placing it across the top of your plate and switch your fork to your right hand. With the tines pointed up, use your fork to lift food to your mouth.

The rest of the world uses the "Continental" style of dining. Begin the same way, holding your fork in your left hand, tines pointed down, and knife in your right hand. Now, cut one bite-sized piece of food, and with tines still pointed down, lift that food to your mouth.

Lots of new professionals from Europe and Asia ask whether they should switch to the American style of dining when working in the United States. And similarly, I've had loads of new professionals in the US ask if they should switch to the Continental style when they travel to Europe. Use whichever style ensures that you successfully move food from your plate to your mouth. However, you should use the American *or* the Continental style—not some hybrid style that you've created on your own.

American-style pause signal

Continental-style pause signal

American-style finished signal

Continental-style finished signal

Let's say that during the course of a discussion over a business meal, you wish to pause and pay particular attention to what someone is saying. Placing your silverware in a particular manner (depending on whether you're using the American or Continental style of dining) silently signals to the waitstaff that you've taken a temporary break from eating. Waiters know they should not clear your plate when your silverware is placed in this manner. See page 53 for illustrations.

If you wish to communicate to the waitstaff that you have completed a particular course and are prepared for it to be cleared from the table, place your silverware in one of the two positions illustrated on page 54.

37. Break bread

With regards to eating bread or dinner rolls, here's the rule: break off a portion equivalent to one or two bites, butter that portion, and then enjoy.

Please avoid the following:

■ Do not use the butter knife to cut a roll in half. Use your butter knife only to spread butter.

■ Do not break a roll in half or take an entire slice of bread and slather butter all over it. Break off and butter just one or two bites that you will eat immediately.

■ Do not move your bread-and-butter plate from its position on the table.

If you are uncertain as to whether a particular bread-and-butter plate belongs to your place setting, your hands can provide the answer. Simply touch your thumbs with the tips of your index fingers, and hold your remaining fingers out straight.

Notice that the fingers of your left hand have formed the letter "b." From now on and forever into the future, that "b" stands for "bread." Your bread plate is always located directly above your left hand. Similarly, notice that the fingers of your right hand have formed the letter "d." From now on and forever into the future, that "d" stands for drink. Your beverage is always located immediately above your right hand.

38. Choose beverages wisely

Although I know the three-martini lunch once existed, I have no idea how the people who participated in those meals completed one whit of work during afternoon hours.

At most business lunches, you should skip alcoholic beverages altogether. Instead, choose fruit juices, soda, iced tea, or water. At a business dinner, feel free to enjoy a glass of wine. (Depending on your locale and the restaurant, a beer may also be appropriate.) However, skip the high-octane cocktails, which may dull your good business judgment. Save those for evenings out with friends.

If you wish to add a squirt of lemon juice to your beverage of choice, before you squeeze, shield the lemon with your other hand. This ensures that you won't squirt a fellow diner.

If you add a packet of sugar or artificial sweetener to your beverage, place any empty packets on the right-hand side of your place setting as near as possible to the edge of the table. When the waitstaff notices the empty packets, they will approach the table and discretely remove them.

39. Handle mistakes gracefully

During the course of a business meal, if you happen to make a mistake, handle it as gracefully as you can.

When a cherry tomato or lettuce leaf jumps off your salad plate, pick it up and return it to your plate, if you can do so discretely.

If breaking bread or a roll produces all sorts of crumbs, leave them. In very nice restaurants, waitstaff will use a small device called a "crumber" to artfully remove them.

If you knock over a beverage, use your napkin to immediately stop the flow of liquid. Then quickly make eye contact with waitstaff and seek their assistance. They will manage the spilled liquid and provide you with a substitute beverage. (By the way, if you're responsible for a spill *and* your spill stains another diner's outfit, you are responsible for their dry-cleaning bill.)

If you drop a piece of silverware or some food on the floor and you believe that someone might trip or slip on it, quickly inform the waitstaff.

If you take a bite of food and suddenly realize that you can't swallow it, use whatever utensil you used to bring the food to your mouth to remove the item and return it to your plate.

40. Work with the waitstaff

Much as support staff can "make you or break you" in the office, waitstaff can help make any business meal into an opportunity for you to advance your career, build a team, or close a deal. As you work to become a regular at several restaurants, build relationships with the host, hostess, and other waitstaff. Should you need a reservation on short notice or should you arrive at a packed restaurant without a reservation, these restaurant professionals can help ensure you are seated quickly and served with decorum.

At a very minimum, treat the waitstaff respectfully. When you place an order, say "please" and "thank you." Although you don't absolutely need to thank waitstaff every time they refill your water glass or deliver a course to your table, why wouldn't you?

Assuming good service, acknowledge the waitstaff's hard work with a gratuity. A 15 percent tip recognizes good service. When the waitstaff exceeds expectations, I generally provide a 20 percent tip. At restaurants where you've become a regular, remember key restaurant professionals with an additional holiday gratuity at the end of the year.

Chapter 5

Use Technology Wisely

As a student or new professional, you need to master a plethora of old and new technologies, and you must do so in a manner that reflects well on your employer. You may already be able to text and tweet with the best of them. However, depending on where you work, you may also need to transmit documents via fax and transfer phone calls on old-fashioned landlines.

Technology helps speed our communications, something that's invaluable in the business world where speed is often of the essence. Unfortunately, when pushed to work fast, many people forget their best manners. They carelessly draft emails and send texts that fail to show concern for the impact a message may have on a recipient. The absence of netiquette can permanently mar important office relationships.

For some business communications, consider avoiding technology altogether. As a student or new professional, you must work to build relationships with your boss and others in the office. Successfully doing so requires that you invest time in connecting face to face. So, switch your smartphone to vibrate, turn off your tablet, and reach out to others for conversations.

41. Determine your boss's preferred means of communication

You may discover that your boss texts just as frequently as you do. On the other hand, you may find that your boss has concluded that important business issues are more readily addressed with a series of quick face-to-face meetings. Make it a point to identify your boss's preferred communication method and adopt it as your own.

Become cognizant of the quantity of information you should share with a particular boss or supervisor. Some bosses are bottom-line oriented. Provide them with solutions and avoid long explanations detailing how you accomplished particular tasks. Other bosses require lots of data and detail. Be prepared to give these supervisors all of the background material you reviewed in developing a response to a particular problem.

When your boss asks you to communicate with clients and customers, make sure that you understand their preferred means of communication, too. Simply ask your employer, "Do you know whether they prefer an email or phone call?"

At the same time, confirm with your employer how you should address the client or customer. In many cases, it will be perfectly fine for you to email clients and customers using their first names. However, in some cases, your boss may prefer that you use the more formal social titles of "Mr." or "Ms." If you are uncertain whether "Pat McNeill" is "Patricia" or "Patrick," get a clarification. Never send a paper or electronic communication that begins, "Dear Mr. or Ms. Pat McNeill."

42. Write effective emails

Beyond the quick face-to-face, serendipitous meetings that occur by chance in the hallway, you will likely find that most business communications occur via email. Ensure that you always communicate in a polite and succinct manner, keeping the following best practices in mind:

- Confirm the email recipient. In many cases, when you begin to type a recipient's name, email software populates the "To" field with anyone and everyone within the organization's database who has the same first name. To avoid sending erroneous emails, before you hit "Send," confirm that the recipient in the "To" field is your intended recipient.

- Create subject lines that accurately describe the nature of the email.

- Think twice before you add a "priority flag" to an email. If you must email about a genuine emergency, by all means use this tool. However, avoid developing a "boy who called wolf" reputation—someone who views all of their own emails as top priority.

- "Cc" and "Bcc" with caution. Many bosses and supervisors receive hundreds of emails per day. Copy them only on messages that they absolutely must see.

- Especially when you initiate an email communication, use a greeting (*Good morning*, *Hello*, or *Dear*) and a sign-off (*Sincerely*, *Regards*, or *All the best*). Without these additional pleasantries, many people interpret emails as orders or demands for action. As an email exchange continues, you can skip the greeting and sign-off.

- Be especially careful when responding to all-office emails, which are generally intended to be informative. If you feel the need to respond, identify the appropriate recipient.

Finally, before you hit "Send," check the tone of your email. Studies consistently find that if recipients can interpret any one word within an email positively, negatively, or neutrally, they'll give it a negative interpretation.

43. Respond to emails

When you respond to emails, be prepared to adjust to the communication expectations of your employer and of any clients or customers with whom you interact.

If you happen to work for an organization in which employees are expected to be connected 24/7, be prepared to respond to all emails within approximately two hours of receiving them. Note: generally, you don't need to provide a final and complete answer within two hours. However, you should acknowledge all emails and provide an estimate as to when you will fully respond. For example, you might respond, "I've received your email regarding the final market comps. I anticipate having those before close of business today. I will follow up with you as soon as they are in hand."

When you receive an email that contains several questions, embed your answers into the email using a different color font to highlight your responses. Out of respect for everyone's time, before you hit "Send," confirm that you've responded to all questions.

"Cc" and "Bcc" with restraint. Copy only those people who absolutely must receive a particular message. If you choose to forward a portion of an email exchange—this may be appropriate where much of an email is not relevant—provide appropriate context.

44. Email professionally

When you initiate and respond to workplace emails, keep your communications professional. Use a professional tone, and ensure that all spelling, punctuation and word usage is business-appropriate.

Several studies have documented that people feel free to make statements in emails and texts that they would never say to another person in a face-to-face conversation. Most attribute this to an absence of visual cues—when people don't see the impact of their comment, they show less restraint in making an emotionally charged remark. As a result, emails have a nasty way of escalating disagreements and disputes.

Remember, any offhand, snarky remark you make in an email can permanently mar a professional relationship. If you have any doubts as to whether you should send a particular message, delete it. If you decide to disregard this advice, at least place the message in a "Drafts" folder for a 24-hour period. Let tempers cool and passions wane. Then, rethink your message.

Finally, never place anything in an email that is insensitive to another person's race, ethnicity, gender, religion, etc. Emails live forever. Something you send in a click can easily be printed and become a permanent part of your employee file.

45. Respect others' private time

I tend to wake at an obscenely early hour each morning. This allows me to attack email and then turn to my most pressing projects long before most people's alarm clocks have buzzed. I also tend to work some portion of nearly every weekend.

Long ago, I became aware that my waking and working habits led me to send emails when others intentionally sought to be off-line. During the course of many weekends and early Monday mornings, I filled others' email inboxes. I felt badly knowing that when others logged in on Monday morning, they had little chance to ease into their workweeks. Instead, they faced my deluge of questions, which I'm certain caused some heads to spin.

Today, when I feel the need to create an email over the weekend or very early on a workday morning, I try to save the email to a "Drafts" folder. Unless I'm scheduled to be out-of-pocket throughout the morning, I wait to send those emails until I feel certain that most intended recipients have arrived in their offices and are comfortably at work.

46. Use caution on any social network

B e extremely cautious about posting online anything that's less than positive about your employer or coworkers. Doing so is bad manners and may place you in violation of your employer's social networking policy.

The same rule applies with regard to posting pictures online.

Even if you have been explicitly hired to blog or tweet, be extremely cautious about your postings. The Internet is replete with examples of job offers withdrawn and job dismissals issued because of an inappropriate message that someone communicated in 140 characters or less.

On occasion, you will feel the need to vent at work. Please do not vent online. Any momentary sense of catharsis you might feel can lead to professional repercussions that will impact your career forever. Instead, breathe deeply or take a walk around the block.

47. Use smartphones and tablets carefully

Increasingly, business communication has moved from desktops and laptops to tablets and smartphones. With some exceptions, many professionals in today's workforce find that they can work anywhere and anytime. However, this freedom brings its own challenges, including knowing when it's appropriate to respond to the messages you receive.

As a new professional, you will likely encounter competing etiquette concerns. For example, when participating in a meeting with coworkers or clients, you know it's rude to glance at your smartphone. Yet, you may work in a culture in which junior employees are expected to be available 24/7. What should you do?

Whenever possible, give your complete attention to the people with whom you meet. This demonstrates that you respect them and their time. It also helps you avoid making critical mistakes. All of us like to believe that we can effectively multitask, but studies consistently find that few people can manage simultaneous face-to-face and electronic communications well. Our capabilities further diminish as a subject matter becomes more complex.

Attempt to focus on one communication at a time. Look for the nuances and unspoken messages that can be critical to comprehension.

48. Speak on the telephone with style

Though you will likely spend more time emailing and texting at work, you should know how to place and receive phone calls with style.

- Create a voicemail message on your landline and smartphone that clearly states your name and the name of your employer. Invite others to leave a message, and promise you will return their call as soon as possible. My voicemail message sounds something like: "Hi, this is Mary Crane. I'm sorry I missed your phone call. Please feel free to leave your name and number. I will return your call as soon as possible."

- When you place a call, show that you respect others' time by knowing exactly what you wish to say or ask. If necessary, create a script and follow it. When your call is answered, quickly introduce yourself and move to the purpose of your call.

- If you place a call, and the person you're calling is unavailable, leave a voicemail message. Clearly articulate your name, your employer, and your phone number. Generally, I indicate that I will take responsibility for following up, saying, "I'll take responsibility for phoning you again later today. However, if it's easier for you to reach out to me, my number is … ."

- When you answer a phone call, use a greeting and state your name. This ensures that your caller immediately knows whom they have reached. By the way, don't bark or growl your greeting. A genuine "hello," "good morning," or "hi" can facilitate conversations and help you build relationships.

49. Make the most of other technologies

As you enter the workforce, you will encounter a plethora of other means of communication. As you use them, always keep others' needs and effective communication in mind.

- When invited to participate in a conference call, unless you are the call's host or have a designated speaking role, plan to listen more than you speak. Arrive fully prepared to contribute relevant information. Be prepared to introduce yourself at the beginning of the call. From that point on, whenever you interject, restate your name so that others know who is speaking. Avoid carrying on any incidental side conversations that might be disruptive.

- When invited to participate in a videoconference or a meeting via Skype, arrive fully prepared to participate. If asked, introduce yourself. Speak clearly and deliberately into the camera. Avoid side conversations. Before you become distracted by your smartphone, realize that all participants will observe your behavior. And since others will see you, wear business-appropriate attire.

- If you host a meeting that will occur over an electronic platform, prepare an agenda and circulate it prior to the meeting. Confirm that people with key speaking roles are fully prepared. Check the meeting environment to ensure that it will not be disrupted by extraneous noise or light. Test all equipment to ensure that everyone, including those in remote locations, will be able to see and hear the entire interaction.

50. Prepare to disconnect professionally

As you progress in your career, you will discover the need to temporarily disconnect from the workplace. Do so. It will help you preserve your sanity, increase your focus, and make you a better employee in the long run.

However, before you go silent, manage your internal and external clients' expectations. Go ahead and plan an out-of-town weekend escape. But before you travel, meet with your supervisor, describe your plans, and confirm that it's acceptable for you to turn off your smartphone— or to check for emergency messages only once a day.

Please do not disconnect from some forms of technology simply because you find them inconvenient. In 2013, a *New York Times* columnist wrote:

Some people are so rude. Really, who sends an email or text message that just says "Thank you"? Who leaves a voicemail message when you don't answer, rather than texting you? Who asks for a fact easily found on Google?

Don't these people realize that they're wasting your time?

Of course, some people might think me the rude one for not appreciating life's little courtesies. But many social norms just don't make sense to people drowning in digital communication.

The column generated a huge amount of attention, with most comments focusing on the author's bad manners. Remember, people with good manners help others feel comfortable. Should your boss or a client feel most comfortable communicating via Morse code, show some good manners and learn how to communicate in dots, dits, and dashes.

Chapter 6

Travel Smart

For many students and new professionals, nothing seems more exciting than the prospect of traveling on an employer's dime. What could be better than someone else picking up the cost of you cross-country airfare, hotel bills, and meals consumed with clients and customers?

Business travel can be exciting. But it can also be exhausting. Trust me on this: nothing will be a greater test of your ability to be polite than beginning the last leg of an excruciatingly long business trip only to encounter multiple flight cancellations and a dearth of available hotel rooms.

Make the most of business travel opportunities. As you pack up your work papers and professional-looking travel clothes, summon up your best manners, too.

51. Plan and prepare for contingencies

Years of experience have taught me to spend a little time trying to imagine what could possibly go wrong on a business trip—and to plan my workarounds.

Before you head out on a business trip, assume something will go wrong. Then create some contingency plans. Long before you travel to the airport, know your options should your flight cancel. Likewise, prepare for the possibility that your hotel may overbook. It's happened to me exactly one time, and boy, was I delighted that I carried a copy of my confirmation. It immediately ended any discussion of fault. Since the hotel had erred, I felt completely comfortable insisting they move me to an alternative hotel of my choice *and* pick up the cost.

Make it easy for airlines, hotels, and the like to help you succeed. When a tropical storm spins in the Caribbean or a polar vortex pushes out of Canada, contact your airline as soon as possible and ask, "Can we change my flight so that I fly a day early? We'd both rather see me arrive early than face a cancelled flight." Generally, the airlines have bent over backwards to help me succeed, moving me to earlier flights at no additional cost.

Avoid last minute dashes to the airport or train station. Nothing creates stress like the business traveler who jumps into a cab and shouts to the driver, "My flight departs in 30 minutes. Let's go!" These travelers place unnecessary pressure on everyone with whom they interact, including TSA agents, gate agents, flight attendants, and the like.

52. Dress professionally

Whenever you travel on business, you represent yourself as well as your employer. As a result, it's important that you dress in a manner that's both business-appropriate and comfortable.

As a general rule, dress according to the business-attire expectations of the company you will visit. Don't assume you'll have adequate time to change from relaxed travel attire to business-appropriate attire. If your trip includes meetings with major Wall Street investors, you should board your flight dressed in a suit. If the trip involves meetings in Silicon Valley, more relaxed attire may be acceptable for both your flight and eventual meetings.

This is true even if your business trip involves a dreaded red-eye flight. Whenever I board an overnight flight, I dress in a business-appropriate outfit. Before I nod off to sleep, I generally switch into a pair of yoga pants and a turtleneck. Then, just before we land, I switch back to business attire.

53. Survive airline travel, part 1

S ince so much business travel involves airline travel, let's spend some time on this topic.

In terms of getting on and off flights, keep the following in mind:

- Arrive at your gate as early as possible and keep one ear open for last minute changes to your departure location. Just last week I encountered a fellow business traveler who missed his flight when he became lost in some work and missed a gate change announcement. An unfortunate lapse was made worse by the fact that we were all traveling late— on that evening, there were no other flights to his destination.

- Board only when your section is called, and please don't push your way into the line.

- If it's sized to fit, place your suitcase or roller board in the overhead bin as close to your seat as possible.

- Please do use the area under the seat in front of you to store smaller items. That gives more travelers access to treasured overhead space.

- If, upon landing, you need to make a very tight connection, work with the flight attendants to be reseated as near to the cabin door as possible. Hurdling seats is not good form.

54. Survive airline travel, part 2

Beyond getting on and off the plane, you should follow some additional rules of good behavior while flying, including the following:

- Remember, the role of the flight attendants is to help you safely travel from one locale to another. They deserve the same level of respect as any other coworker. When they speak, give them your attention, even when you're about to hear the safety instructions for the millionth time.

- Let's agree that people assigned to the dreaded middle seats have earned the armrests—no more fighting over them.

- Before you recline an airline seat, ask for permission or tell the person behind you what you're about to do.

- If you have brought a child along on business travel, you are responsible for your child's behavior. Do not allow her to kick the back of the seat in front of her or scream at the top of her lungs. The rest of us need to give the wee ones a break, remembering we were once disruptive children, too.

55. Leave transportation lavatories as clean as you found them

There's no delicate way to handle this, so I'll be blunt. If you travel for any length of time on a bus, train, or plane, you may need to use the lavatory. Keep in mind that you share those facilities with dozens, if not hundreds of other travelers. You have an absolute responsibility to leave a lavatory in as good shape as you found it.

The same holds true for public restrooms in airports, train and bus stations, and highway rest stations.

Anyone seated in an aisle seat has an obligation to graciously accommodate the needs of other travelers when they ask to use the facilities.

56. Travel by train

When you travel by train, as with air travel, you should arrive at your gate with time to spare, board when you're called to do so, and work with your fellow travelers to make the trip as easy as possible for all concerned.

Train travel does give rise to a few unique concerns, including the following:

- Most business travelers are now accustomed to being crammed onto flights that are filled to capacity. With the exception of holiday travel, I generally find trains less likely to be jam-packed. It's one of the reasons I prefer them: oftentimes I can spread out. Nonetheless, when trains are filled, riders should store their luggage and work papers appropriately so that others may sit in unoccupied seats.

- Should you receive a phone call while traveling by train, make sure you use your "inside voice." Be particularly careful not to discuss confidential information. If you have taken a seat in a "quiet car," move to an exit before you receive or place a phone call.

- Perform all personal grooming activities before you board the train or in the train lavatory. Ladies, please do not sit in the café car and apply your makeup; and gentlemen, please do not stand at one end of the train and use your electric razor.

57. Act like the perfect hotel guest

When traveling on business, recognize those hotel employees who make your stay comfortable. Plan on leaving the following gratuities:

- **Doormen and bellhops** – $2 per bag, $2 to $5 when they flag a taxi for you.

- **Room service** – A gratuity is generally included in the room service bill; however, when someone hurries to my room with a desperately needed early morning pot of coffee, I often thank the server with an additional $5 tip.

- **Maid service** – Except for the kitchen staff, the housekeeping staff is among the hardest working group of people in any hotel. Leave $3 to $5 on your pillow each morning before you depart for the day.

- **Concierge** – These people are your local experts. They can help you secure a reservation at the perfect restaurant for your business meetings. They can even help you find the perfect last-minute business gift. Your tip should vary according to the amount of effort the concierge expends.

Beyond recognizing the staff, remain cognizant of other hotel guests. Many hotel rooms are not soundproof. When conducting in-room meetings or phone calls, be aware of the volume of your voice. Avoid slamming doors. Monitor the volume of TVs, CD players, your personal technology, and the like.

58. Work professionally in a visitor's office

While on business travel, you may need to work as a visitor in another office. In many cases, a host office will provide you with a private area in which to work. In these cases, quickly introduce yourself to the receptionist and to any other support staff with whom you interact.

As soon as possible, acclimate yourself to the rules—spoken and unspoken—of the office. To avoid constantly interrupting others, find the location of the nearest restroom, refreshment station, copy machine, printer, and so forth.

Ensure that your key contacts within the organization know your location.

Unless you have been invited to wander freely, stay close to your assigned workspace. Never assume that you have unfettered access to other areas of an office.

59. Travel internationally

We have fully moved into a global economy. Consequently, today's students and new professionals face the prospect of working with many people who come from cultures far different from their own.

When traveling internationally for work, try to assimilate to other cultures as quickly as possible. If you travel to a more formal culture, adopt a more formal demeanor (see #85).

Be especially cognizant of your body language. Understand that hand gestures and foot placement common in the United States may be interpreted as an insult in another culture (see #84).

If your employer has offices in other countries, view your international coworkers as important sources of information. Generally, they will be delighted to explain their culture and its nuances. Be open to their instruction.

At a very minimum, learn how to say "please" and "thank you" in the language of every country you visit. Even when you struggle to articulate these words correctly, people within your host country will appreciate the efforts you make.

60. Develop some patience

Years ago, I was scheduled to take a red-eye flight from San Francisco International Airport to Washington, DC's Dulles Airport. Anyone who travels in and out of San Francisco knows that SFO frequently crawls to a standstill due to encroaching fog, which is exactly what occurred on that evening.

Around 9:00 p.m., airlines began cancelling flights, and they continued to do so into the late evening hours. My airline assured me that my flight would depart, but as the hours marched on, we remained on the ground.

Sometime around midnight, I walked toward my gate and saw a spectacle that I have never forgotten. A business traveler leaned over the gate agent's podium, pressed his face as close to the agent's as possible, and yelled at the top of his voice, "You've got to get me out of here! This flight has got to leave!" He genuinely looked like he was about to explode.

In as calm of a voice as she could muster, the agent explained that she had no control over the weather. The evening's fog had thus far made it impossible for our pilot's flight to land. The airline was in search of a substitute pilot, and she assured my fellow traveler, that as soon as a pilot and crew arrived, our flight would depart. Within the hour, that's exactly what occurred.

Here's what I learned that evening: displaying bad manners rarely alters a situation for the better. Avoid becoming upset over things you cannot control. Instead, when you schedule a business trip, plan for things to go wrong and act with polite wonderment when your trip goes perfectly.

Chapter 7

Manage Office Parties & Other Social Events

As a new professional, you will work incredibly long hours. After all, you have a tremendous amount to learn. In addition to tackling a series of day-to-day tasks, you'll need to adjust to your boss, understand the inner workings of the office, and begin to comprehend the intricacies of a particular industry. In a matter of months, you'll perform quickly and efficiently. Until then, don't be surprised to find that you require an inordinate amount of time to craft a single paragraph or complete a simple financial analysis.

That's not to say that students and new professionals experience all work and no play. As you enter the world of work, you will be invited to a plethora of social events. It's critically important that you attend these. Every event affords you the opportunity to begin building a series of invaluable business relationships.

Attend as many business-social events as your schedule permits. Just keep in mind that these are first and foremost *business* events, requiring that you always act and speak in a business-appropriate manner.

61. Respond to invitations

As soon as you receive an invitation to a business-social event, check your calendar and confirm your availability. If possible, respond to invitations as they arrive. Should a partner send an early morning email in which he or she invites you to lunch, please do not delay responding in hopes that you will receive a "better offer."

If an invitation requests your response (*RSVP*), contact the host or hostess immediately and convey whether you will attend. Once you have indicated that you will attend, only an absolute emergency excuses your absence. Remember, your host will purchase food and beverage based on the *RSVPs* received. It's extremely poor manners to cause your host to spend money needlessly.

Should you receive invitations for two events on the same evening, it's perfectly okay to piggyback one event on the other. Whenever possible, give precedence to the event to which you were initially invited and attend it first. At the halfway point, thank the hostess and express your apologies for your need to depart early. Then, scoot on off to your second event.

62. Dress appropriately

In general, when social events are scheduled immediately before, during, or after normal work hours, office attire is appropriate. Depending on the industry in which you work, this may vary from conservative to business-casual. Always dress professionally. (In most cases, this means no sundresses, no T-shirts, and no torn jeans.) Senior people within the organization, as well as clients and customers, will observe your appearance and make snap decisions as to whether you fit in.

A good rule of thumb: dress for the job you want to have. If you hope to become a senior partner in a New York City law firm, observe the attire of the most successful partners and dress in a similar manner. If you hope to enter the world of Silicon Valley's thought leaders, don't automatically assume that a hoody and jeans are the norm.

If the invitation you receive to a business-social event specifies attire, adhere to those instructions. If an invitation specifies "black tie," please do not arrive wearing jeans and a T-shirt. Instead, gentlemen should wear a tux and ladies a long dress.

63. Prepare

To make the most of business-social events, invest some time beforehand preparing for the event. At a minimum, plan to undertake the following:

- **Prepare your introduction.**
  Know how you will introduce yourself and describe the work you do. Make your introduction memorable. View it as your own 30-second commercial. Remember, you will have only one opportunity to meet the CEO or managing partner for the first time, so make it good.

- **Develop some conversation starters.**
  Formulate three to five questions that you can ask anyone who attends the event. If you are an introvert, these questions are an absolute lifesaver. Most people love to talk about themselves, so ask questions that allow others to shine. Doing so will position you as a brilliant conversationalist.

- **Gather your supplies.**
  Since you never know when you'll meet an important new contact—even within your own organization—and wish to exchange contact information, always carry your business cards with you. Take along a pen so that you can add a handwritten note to your card before exchanging it.

- **Grab a snack.**
  Avoid arriving at any business-social event on an empty stomach. Rather than quieting a grumbling stomach, stay focused on connecting with others.

64. Arrive on time

One urban dictionary defines "fashionably late" as "the refined art of being just late enough (5 minutes or so) to give the impression that you are a busy, popular person who was held up with other business."

People with good manners do not focus on conveying the impression that they are "busy" or "popular."

Whenever possible, arrive at events on time. Most hosts and hostesses understand delays of 10 or 15 minutes. (Who hasn't been unavoidably stuck in traffic?) However, when you arrive late by 20 minutes or more, you communicate to your host or hostess that the event was not a top priority—you didn't plan for the possibility of a delay. Also, you have likely missed out on the opportunity to make a new connection or two.

If you are an introvert, arrive as close to the starting time as possible. Introverts know that few things feel more intimidating than walking into a room packed with people. Since fewer people will be present at the event's start, calmly arrive on time and find your first conversation.

When you arrive, find the host or hostess and thank them for their invitation.

65. Arrive at someone's home

Business-social events may be conducted within the confines of an office or any number of other locations, including restaurants, hotel ballrooms, and private clubs. When you are invited to a business-social event hosted in someone's home, it's especially important for you to take your very best manners with you.

Bring a host/hostess gift. Your gift should reflect your understanding of your host's interests. If your hostess is a student of political history, she might appreciate Doris Kearns Goodwin's latest write-up. If your host is a baseball fan, he might appreciate a signed baseball cap. If you're uncertain about their interests, flowers are almost always appropriate, as is a gift basket filled with special treats.

Never bring an uninvited guest. If it's a working event and spouses or significant others have not been invited, your new girlfriend or boyfriend may not tag along. The same rule applies to children. When family members have been invited, parents are responsible for their children's behavior.

Afterward, send a handwritten thank-you note. Convey your special appreciation for having been welcomed into someone's home. Send your note to the host or hostess's home address.

66. Manage beverage consumption

At many business-social events, especially those conducted after work hours, alcohol may be served. Bottom line: know your limits and don't exceed them.

Every company, firm, and governmental agency has within its organizational memory some story about a professional who consumed too much alcohol and then said or did something that permanently affected a career. Don't become that person!

As soon as you arrive at a business-social event, go to the bar, request a beverage (alcoholic or nonalcoholic), and hold it in your left hand. This will keep your hands positioned at waist level, which will help you look welcoming and approachable. By holding your beverage in your left hand, your right hand will always be available to greet others.

At most business-social events, skip cocktails made with high-octane alcohol. It's way too easy for the alcohol to affect your good business judgment.

If for any reason you choose to abstain from alcohol altogether, that's perfectly fine. Please don't let anyone force you into drinking a beverage that you do not want. If a polite "no thanks" doesn't stop a coworker from pushing a drink on you, come up with a polite excuse; for example, "I'd love to have a martini, but I need to complete a market segmentation analysis tonight. May I take a rain check?"

67. Manage the buffet table

As a rule of thumb, I avoid the buffet table at most business-social events. I attend events knowing it may be my one-and-only opportunity to meet some other key attendee. When I introduce myself to that person and extend my right hand for a handshake, I want to ensure that my hand is neat and clean, something that won't be the case if I've just nibbled a greasy or sticky canapé. So, I generally grab a beverage and completely skip the food offerings.

Should you opt to grab a bite at a business-social event, look for food options that will leave your hands as neat and clean as possible. Avoid anything that's obviously sticky, laden with sauce, or gooey. If some food item is sitting in a puddle of oil or grease, you probably want to walk away.

Above all, do not hold a beverage and a plate of nibbles at the same time. Keep your right hand available to meet and greet others. So grab something to drink *or* something to eat, but never both.

68. Mingle

Business-social events afford you the opportunity to meet coworkers, clients and customers, as well as other people who share an interest in a particular industry or cause. Use these opportunities to connect and build relationships. As I often remind my clients, you never know who you'll meet on any given day, nor can you predict the opportunities that person may create for you. Be open to the possibilities.

If the event is strictly internal—one to which only employees have been invited—make sure you connect with the people with whom you work. Catch up on a social level, leaving your day-to-day work problems behind. Then, move beyond your normal circle of coworkers and mingle. Meet people in other departments and practice groups. Establish connections. Identify opportunities for cooperation and growth.

Uncertain who to approach for your first conversation? If you're at a complete loss, look for the most miserable-looking person in the room—the person standing alone along the perimeter of the room or near the buffet table. You'll be amazed at how many very successful people are less than comfortable in a roomful of people. They will genuinely appreciate you initiating a 10- or 15-minute conversation with them. So walk up and introduce yourself.

Avoid monopolizing any one person's time. Please do not latch onto someone for the entire business-social event. Share a brief, pleasant conversation and then move on.

69. Choose appropriate conversation content

At many business-social events, especially those conducted in the workplace, people have a tendency to lapse into "shop talk." While there's nothing wrong with addressing a genuine work emergency, keep business talk to a minimum. These events are intended for participants to connect socially.

Of course, it's never wrong to recognize a special success. So if someone has just sealed the deal on a billion-dollar contract or settled a multimillion-dollar lawsuit, by all means, offer your congratulations.

Above all, do not whine or complain during a business-social event. Conversations about grievances or perceived slights should be reserved for a nonsocial meeting.

Keep your conversations business-appropriate. Say nothing that others might find offensive, especially comments about race, religion, sexual preference, or identity. Avoid subject matters that evoke strong emotions. Use these opportunities to position yourself as an intelligent new professional with a bright future.

70. Express your appreciation

You will never err by thanking someone for an invitation to a business-social event.

At the end of a business lunch, thank the person who hosted the meal. In most cases, a verbal "thank you" should suffice. However, if the business lunch capped off an interview, you should follow up with a handwritten note.

You should also send a handwritten thank-you note after a business dinner, especially if the dinner took place at the home of your host or hostess. Acknowledge the special effort made to help you feel welcome. In such a case, the note should be mailed to the host's home address. If the dinner was conducted at a restaurant, the letter may be sent to the host's business address.

Following a reception, send a handwritten thank-you note to your host and hostess. If you're focused on building your professional network—and why wouldn't you be?—send at least three follow-up emails to people you met at the reception and start the process of converting your new contacts into valued members of your network.

Chapter 8

Gift with Style

Selecting a gift for a boss, colleague, or client might seem like the type of carefree activity that you can put off until the very last minute. Don't make this mistake. Gifting coworkers and clients requires careful thought and consideration.

Even international etiquette professionals have been known to make serious gift giving errors. Long after she served as Jacqueline Kennedy's White House Social Secretary, Letitia Baldrige disclosed her own nearly disastrous gift giving *faux pas*.

Prior to the First Lady's 1962 solo journey to India and Pakistan, Baldrige purchased 150 exquisite frames from Tiffany's for Mrs. Kennedy to present to various high-level officials. Moments before the delegation departed Washington, someone realized that the gifts were all made of leather. Presenting these frames in India, where the cow is sacred, would have offended every recipient. Fortunately, Baldrige caught the error, contacted the Army Signal Corps by radio, and had 150 silver frames immediately dispatched east.

Select business gifts thoughtfully and present them in a manner that reflects your respect for the recipient and his or her position.

71. Know the rules

Many organizations have created explicit rules about giving and receiving gifts. Go to great lengths to understand those rules. When you have questions, your recipient's human resources department—or in the case of government officials, an ethics office—should be able to clarify them.

When you find that an organization prohibits gifts of any kind, adhere to both the letter and spirit of the prohibition. Do not give physical gifts, and do not extend invitations to special events such as the Super Bowl, a night at the theater, or a vacation. This principle applies even when you've established a personal friendship above and beyond a professional relationship.

When an organization has established a culture in which gift giving is frowned upon but not forbidden, act with caution. In situations where you have established a personal relationship with a colleague and wish to acknowledge it with a gift, take your gift exchange outside the office.

The same rule holds true when you wish to gift one person in the office to the exclusion of everyone else. Do your gifting privately.

72. Select business gifts with care

Whether you are acting as a Secret Santa for a member of the company's administrative staff or wish to thank a client for her ongoing business, show both thoughtfulness and restraint in selecting gifts.

By all means, avoid the following:

- anything that is too personal in nature, including lingerie, perfume, and jewelry;

- gag gifts, since you can never assume that a recipient will understand your intended humor; and

- anything of a religious nature, unless, of course, you work for a religious institution.

Before giving gifts to international clients or colleagues, research relevant cultures. Understand that something as simple as the color of wrapping paper may have implications. For example, while you may enjoy the stark simplicity of plain white paper, this color is viewed as a symbol of mourning in China.

Also, before you send gifts of food or wine, good manners dictate that you know something about the eating and drinking habits of the recipient. You probably don't want to send a crate of steaks to a vegetarian and you definitely don't want to send a case of scotch to someone who abstains from alcohol.

73. Gift a client

Generally, senior people within organizations are tasked with determining which clients should receive gifts—and the nature of those gifts. However, if you've joined a startup with a relatively flat hierarchical structure, your input may be requested.

In general, keep the following in mind:

- Many organizations currently prohibit the receipt of any gift valued at $25 or more.

- If you wish to give a gift of greater value, contact the intended recipient's human resources department and confirm their gift policies. Avoid placing a recipient in the position of needing to return a gift.

- When you are in the midst of negotiating a deal or bidding for work, never even think about giving a gift to a prospective client or customer. Avoid creating the scenario in which your holiday gift may be interpreted as an attempt to seal the deal.

74. Receive gifts

If you are the recipient of a business gift, you too need to show caution.

If your organization has specific gift rules, confirm that any gift you receive falls within approved parameters. If you have any uncertainty, take the gift to Human Resources and confirm that the gift does not violate any rules.

If HR tells you the gift violates established policies, return the gift with a nice handwritten note explaining why you need to return the gift, and thanking the giver for the sentiments.

If you may keep the gift and it's comprised of a food basket or a case of wine, think about sharing the gift with others in the office. Doing so demonstrates that you recognize the contributions they've made to this business relationship. Sharing can also help build morale.

When family members exchange gifts, participants often hang onto receipts just in case the recipient wishes to exchange a gift for a different size or color. In the case of a business gift, please never request a return receipt.

75. Gift your boss

As a rule of thumb, never gift up.

Others may view your gift to the boss as an attempt to "suck up" and possibly to receive special favors or prime assignments. If you wish to express your appreciation to your boss for the opportunities he or she has afforded you, schedule a one-on-one conversation or write a classy note.

If an entire team decides to gift a boss, every member of the team must voluntarily agree to participate in the gift giving. No one should feel as if his or her job depends on participation, and everyone's personal budget should be kept in mind when asking for contributions.

If your boss gifts you, please do not feel the need to reciprocate. Instead, handwrite a thank-you note expressing your appreciation.

76. Gift support staff

You will almost never err by showing your appreciation to the support staff who help you successfully launch your career. A small token of appreciation helps you recognize the receptionist who welcomes your clients to the office or the mailroom clerk who speeds your documents to a judge's chambers.

When selecting gifts for staff, adhere to the rules of your organization, especially regarding any prescribed limits on the value of gifts.

Avoid any gift that may be viewed as too personal in nature (see #72). Ideally, your gift to a member of the support team should be usable in the business setting. That generally means desk accessories: for example, a frame for a family photo or an attractive paperweight may be appropriate for your administrative assistant. If he or she carries a caramel macchiato into the office each morning, you might consider a gift card to the local coffee shop.

77. Gift to a charity in lieu of

Many businesses and other organizations have identified specific charities they support. In lieu of giving a physical gift, consider giving the gift of time. Your commitment to roll up your sleeves and work side by side at a food bank or as part of a disaster relief effort may make a far greater impression than a $25 token of your appreciation. Besides, this affords you an additional opportunity to strengthen your client relationship.

If you don't know which charities your intended gift recipient supports, you have a new reason to have a face-to-face conversation with your contact. Successful business people constantly focus on relationship building. So use this conversation to deepen your relationship with a client, customer or colleague.

Before you give a gift to a charity in a client or colleague's name, confirm their interest in that particular cause. Some people are extremely selective when it comes to attaching their names to specific causes. Avoid linking someone to a cause without his or her full support.

78. Gift as a startup

If you're a new professional who has launched a startup, gift giving can be particularly important. Your end-of-the-year gifts can serve two purposes:

- They can thank important clients and customers for their business; and

- They can create a buzz about your company.

Like every other business, a startup must adhere to gift limitations imposed by an intended recipient's policies. If policies cap the value of any gift at $25, keep this in mind when selecting a gift.

Similarly, a startup should avoid gifts that are too personal in nature (see #72).

In terms of gift giving, startups do have a little extra leeway on one front: although most business professionals should avoid gifts that bear a corporate logo, a startup may be able to get away with this. Just keep the display of the logo tasteful and discrete.

79. In general, do not gift government officials

Students and new professionals who launch their careers in government service must toe the line when it comes to receiving any sort of gift. A misunderstanding as to the nature of a gift or a miscalculation regarding the value of the gift may have serious repercussions, not only for the new professional, but also for the government official for whom he or she works.

In general, the rules are as follows:

- Employees are prohibited from giving gifts to "an official superior" and from accepting gifts from another employee who receives less pay.

- Employees are prohibited from seeking or accepting gifts from "prohibited sources."

- Employees are prohibited from accepting payments from nongovernmental sources.

When in doubt, check with the relevant ethics office.

80. Thank others for their gifts

Assuming a gift is legal and consistent with organizational policy, your appropriate response upon receiving a gift is to express a simple and genuine verbal "thanks." Just say, "Thank you. I appreciate your thoughtfulness," or "Thank you. How kind of you to think of me."

If you wish to make a positive impression, follow your verbal thanks with a brief handwritten note. To write the perfect thank-you note, craft three simple sentences.

Dear (fill in the blank),

Thank you very much for the gift.
Describe something that makes the gift memorable.
Include a brief statement of follow-up.

Sincerely,

Your name

So I might write to a vendor:

Dear Wilhelm,

Thank you so much for the lovely selection of Christmas cookies you delivered to our office. Everyone enjoyed them, especially me who grew up feasting on linzer cookies throughout my childhood holidays. We very much look forward to working with you in the New Year.

Sincerely,

Mary

Please do not feel that you must respond to a gift with a gift-in-kind.

Chapter 9

Work Globally with Grace

We have now fully moved into a global economy, and as a result, students and new professionals will interact with cultures from around the world. To be successful on the global stage, you must understand and respect the cultural differences that exist. Failure to do so can yield enormous consequences.

Several years ago, a partner at a prestigious law firm told me how that entity's litigation group had managed to lose a multimillion-dollar client. Based in Japan, the client team had flown the better part of a day to reach Chicago. When the team arrived, they anticipated sitting down for a long dinner with the litigators. Discussing the case was important. But from a cultural perspective, the Japanese team was far more interested in building a relationship with their American lawyers.

According to the partner, when he told his fellow litigators that they needed to step away from trial preparation to attend the dinner, he met with resistance. These brilliant lawyers failed to recognize the cultural implications of not connecting with their client.

When you work globally, be prepared to adjust the way you interact with colleagues and clients alike.

81. Learn from your international colleagues

When you work with a business that operates on the international stage, make an effort to learn from your colleagues who are based abroad. Observe their behaviors and adjust your own based on what you see. If they act in a more formal manner, you should do the same.

Some years ago, I delivered a presentation on networking skills to members of an international law firm. As part of my presentation, I discussed how to properly introduce oneself. Because I do a lot of my work within the United States, I mentioned that Americans often decide quickly that they know each other well enough to use first names.

Following the presentation, a contingent from the firm's Munich and Frankfurt offices approached me to say that using someone's first name on their home turf would be considered forward and brash. One lawyer explained that, despite working together for many years, he still addressed several of his male colleagues using the social title of "Herr."

When you work globally, study the cultural norms of the people with whom you interact and take their lead.

82. Prepare to dress conservatively

Unless business travel takes you to a Paris couture show, pack conservative attire for most international business trips. Never assume that business-casual attire will be appropriate. Depending on the industry in which you work, this likely means that you should pack several suits.

It's critical that all of your attire demonstrates respect for the culture in which you will work. For example, if business travel takes you to the Middle East, men and women should wear clothing that loosely covers. Avoid exposing your shoulders, arms and legs. Also, avoid open-toed shoes. Women should pack a Pashmina shawl or scarf to cover their hair where appropriate.

Remember, when selecting business attire, your primary goal is to fit in. So, understand how your clients and colleagues will dress and choose similar attire.

83. Learn the language

In general, English has become the language of business communication. You will find that many international businesspeople are—if not fluent in English—at least able to converse.

To the extent that you can communicate with others in their native tongue, you will facilitate business exchanges. However, if you are not fluent, be extremely careful in your choice of words—any one of which may carry multiple meanings.

As previously mentioned (see #59), whenever you travel internationally, learn to say "please" and "thank you" in the local dialect. Learning to say "good morning" and "good evening" is a smart move, too.

84. Watch your body language

When working internationally, nonverbal communication becomes extremely important. A hand gesture commonly used in the United States as an indication that everything is perfectly fine (using thumb and forefinger circled together to communicate "okay") is offensive in certain parts of the world where the gesture refers to a body part that's behind you. Similarly, while most Americans would interpret a thumbs-up gesture to mean all is well, that same gesture is viewed as rude and offensive in other parts of the world.

In addition to hand gestures, be aware of the following:

- **Eye contact** – In the United States, greetings typically involve a brief handshake and steady eye contact. The same will not be the case in much of Asia, especially Japan and China, where bows are still common and eye contact tends to be less intense.

- **Feet** – In the United States, it's not uncommon for businesspeople to adopt a relaxed sitting posture, in which legs are crossed. In other parts of the world, respectful businesspeople sit more rigidly with both feet firmly planted on the ground. In some countries, showing the soles of one's feet is a major insult.

- **Touching** – Beyond a handshake, in general, it's best to avoid touching anyone of either gender in the international workplace. However, be aware that you may see businessmen and women exchange "cheek kisses" throughout parts of Europe. And in the Middle East, don't be surprised to see businessmen holding hands.

85. Address others formally

Until you know the norms of a particular workplace or culture, address business colleagues formally. When you greet someone:

- Use social titles (in the United States that would be "Mr." or "Ms.").

- Do not use someone's first name until you are specifically invited to do so. Once the invitation is extended, immediately switch to the more informal exchange.

- Avoid intense, extended eye contact unless you know intense eye contact is the cultural norm.

- Allow others to initiate discussions of topics involving their personal lives or personal matters.

86. Dine internationally

Because so much international business is conducted over meals, it's important to understand some of the rules that govern the global table, including the following:

- **Holding silverware** – You already know that many Americans use the zigzag style of dining while much of the remainder of the world has adopted the Continental style (see #36). When traveling abroad, if you are most comfortable with the American style, do not feel obligated to switch.

- **Pausing** – During the course of a meal in the United States, when diners pause, they typically rest their hands in their laps. In other parts of the world, when pausing, diners rest their forearms against the edge of the table so that their hands are displayed at all times.

- **Deciding how much to eat** – If I were to invite you to my home for dinner, I would be thoroughly complimented to see you eat every morsel of food upon your plate. I would interpret this as a sign that you truly enjoyed the meal. In other parts of the world, "cleaning your plate" communicates that your host provided an insufficient amount of food.

- **Timing business discussions** – In the United States, we generally delay business discussions until after food has been ordered (see #34). Prior to that moment, diners connect socially. In some other parts of the world, business issues are raised before or after—but not during—the course of a meal.

- **Offering to pay for the meal** – Whoever hosts a meal pays for it. When you extend an invitation to dine, you assume the responsibility for its cost. How much a guest may attempt to intervene varies around the world. If you are the host, avoid conflict by visiting the restaurant before a scheduled meal and making arrangements to handle the bill. (Leave your credit card number and ask management to add a customary tip.) Alternatively, before the meal ends, slip away from the table, give your credit card to the maître d' and request that the meal be charged to it.

- **Tipping** – The rules for tipping vary by country, region, and scenario. In some countries, the tip is included in the bill, and the host may leave a small additional amount per guest. In other countries, the host leaves a standard 15 to 20 percent tip and may also tip the maître d' for superlative service.

87. Exchange business cards

In the United States we exchange business cards almost as if we were trading baseball cards: it's a relaxed and informal ritual, with cards quickly dropped into a handbag, portfolio, or pocket.

In other parts of the world, the business card exchange is more ceremonial. In such cases, business cards are viewed as a representation of the individual. For example, in Japan a card is presented with both hands. You should show deference by receiving the card in both hands and by spending a moment or two looking at it. Then place it on the conference room table in front of you for the duration of the meeting. At the end of the meeting, place the business card in a nice card case and never in your back rear pocket.

Throughout much of the Middle East, avoid presenting your business card with your left hand, which is viewed as unclean.

88. Consume alcohol carefully

Be prepared to observe different alcohol consumption habits around the world.

- In Russia, vodka remains a drink of choice. Guests may be offered shots to help establish and build closer relationships.

- In France, a cocktail before a meal may be frowned upon because of a general view that alcohol affects one's ability to taste the food that will follow.

- In many parts of the Middle East, alcohol will be unavailable because of existing religious bans.

So before you order an alcoholic beverage, understand the cultural norms. If the local culture promotes drinking as a means of bonding, by all means feel free to enjoy a pint of beer, a glass of wine, or a sip of the local brew. However, limit your consumption to an amount that ensures your good judgment will not be impaired. And if you choose not to drink alcohol, adhere to your decision.

89. Gift internationally

In international transactions, gifting can be extremely important. The right gift can show your appreciation, enhance your reputation, and cement an important business relationship.

However, it's extremely important to understand local cultural norms regarding business gifts. Some cultures view gifts as an expected social gesture that's deeply rooted in tradition. Other cultures view business gifts as the equivalent of a bribe. Before you gift, know the rules of the country as well as the dictates of the specific business recipient.

Keep in mind the following:

- **Gifts** – Business gifts should reflect the nature of the business relationship. Avoid anything that is personal in nature. Ideally, select high quality gifts that are portable—that can be carried away easily. Before selecting a gift, carefully research the recipient's culture, understanding that different cultures may view the same gift quite differently. For example, one culture may interpret the gift of flowers as a sign of affection while another may view the same flowers as a symbol of death.

- **Wrapping paper** – Some cultures place a high level of importance on extravagant wrapping efforts. Paper selection, especially in terms of color, can be very important. For instance, in some cultures death is associated with the color black; in other cultures, death is associated with the color white.

- **Recipients** – In general, gifts should be presented to the most senior person. If you plan to gift multiple people, a slightly more extravagant gift should be given to the most senior person. In some cases, recipients will open their gifts in your presence. In other cultures, doing so is viewed as bad taste.

- **Logos** – In general, avoid giving gifts bearing corporate logos, which many cultures view as pretentious.

And please don't be surprised when a gift is initially rejected. In some cultures, a recipient is expected to reject a gift three times before he or she accepts it.

90. Blend in

At the very beginning of this book, we discussed the importance of accommodating others. Remember, the person who exhibits good manners always remains aware of the wants and needs of other people and looks for opportunities to ensure their comfort.

Students and new professionals demonstrate their understanding of business etiquette when they study the culture of a business or firm and work hard to fit in. They dress in a manner that is consistent with that culture. They speak in an appropriate manner. They act more or less conservatively based on the dictates of the culture. They know that behaving in such a manner ensures the comfort of their colleagues and employer.

Fitting in becomes especially important when you work on the international stage. As you begin to interact with colleagues and clients from around the world, take the time to learn everything you can about their cultures and take into account their cultural norms whenever possible.

Chapter 10

Miscellaneous

Over the years, students and new professionals have asked me hundreds, if not thousands, of business etiquette questions that don't fit neatly into a designated category. I love these questions. They constantly remind me that today's workforce entrants genuinely want to behave properly.

So what trips you up? Do you hold the door for your supervisor or walk through? Does the gender of the supervisor make a difference? When you attend a business lunch and the waitstaff delivers an entrée that you simply don't like, may you ask for a substitute? When a coworker exhibits a strange body odor in the office day after day, should you confront him or her?

For answers to these and other questions, read on!

91. Walk down the street with style

When men and women walk down the street together, does it matter who walks curbside? It's hardly a life-or-death issue, but even today, it's nice when a thoughtful gentleman places himself between a potentially crazy bicycle messenger and the lady with whom he is walking.

This custom goes all the way back to Medieval times—as do so many of the other more formal rules of etiquette.

Here's the situation our forebears tried to address: Imagine a fancy principality in Medieval Europe. Now imagine a gentleman and a lady scurrying together from one social event to another. Should they walk beneath a window at the very moment in which a maid emptied a chamber pot, positioning the lady nearest the house lessened her chances of becoming a splattered mess.

Additionally, should a horse and carriage pass the couple, a gentleman walking curbside could block possible splashes from the lady with whom he was walking.

92. Hold doors and walk through

The formal rules of social etiquette dictate that a gentleman should always hold a door for a lady. However, people with good manners at work—men and women alike—look for opportunities to help others. If you see someone walking down a hallway with their arms obviously filled with paperwork, by all means, offer to hold the door for that person. The same principle applies when you and a coworker travel on business together. If one person approaches an office toting a computer bag and a suitcase and the other carries a tablet, the person whose hands are most free should hold the door for his or her colleague—regardless of gender.

Ladies, when a gentleman holds a door for you, for heaven's sake, walk through and thank him for his kindness.

As to revolving doors, the social rules dictate that when a gentleman and lady approach together, the gentleman should take control of the door, saying, "Please, allow me to push this for us." This rule is predicated on a belief that the gentleman, probably the stronger of the two, can more easily handle the door and assist the lady with her exit.

93. Ascend in an elevator

While waiting to board an elevator, stand slightly away from the elevator doors so that anyone on board can readily exit before you jump in. This applies especially during morning and evening rush hours.

Once you board the elevator, be aware of others who may be approaching. When it's possible, hold the elevator for them. Your colleagues will appreciate your attention and your efforts to speed them on their way.

Please do not hold an elevator while you and another rider complete a conversation, especially when this delays others.

If you stand near the control panel, offer to push buttons for occupants heading to other floors.

Recognize others with a simple greeting and give them as much space as practicable.

When you arrive at your floor, exit quickly. If you are positioned near the front of the elevator and someone in the rear needs to depart, step out of the elevator and make way for that person to exit. Then, quickly return to your position.

When you encounter an escalator, traditionally men board first.

94. Treat special needs people with respect

It's not always obvious when someone has a special need. Anyone with good manners would offer to hold a door for someone using a wheelchair. However, that same polite person may not know that a client or colleague has a speech impediment until he or she begins to speak.

When you encounter someone with a special need:

- Speak directly to that person—not to a companion who might be accompanying him or her. Address the person with the same respect you show when communicating with other colleagues, friends, and family members.

- Always ask if you may be of assistance before you act. Do not touch someone's wheelchair unless you are invited to do so. If you work with someone who is visually impaired, ask if you may offer assistance across a street or down a hallway. Then, offer your arm for them to hold onto.

- When working with a hearing impaired colleague, position yourself in front of your colleague and speak slowly and clearly—not loudly. When working with a colleague who uses a wheelchair, move to a seated position so that the two of you speak face to face.

- When working with someone with a speech challenge, be patient and allow the person to speak. When you don't understand something the person has said, clarify. Whenever possible ask questions that can be answered succinctly, with a "yes," "no," or head nod.

- When planning events, keep the needs of others in mind. If you anticipate a particular challenge— for example, the main entrance to a ballroom has stairs, though a secondary entrance is wheelchair accessible—forewarn any colleague who uses a wheelchair so he or she can plan for the challenge.

If you have a special need, please understand that most of your colleagues, when they offer assistance, do so with the best of intentions. Accept or reject those offers with grace.

95. Think before telling jokes

People with good manners avoid anything—including attempts at humor—that might be perceived as racist, sexist, or otherwise intolerant. They are sensitive to the emotional state of the people who surround them and recognize that what might seem funny one day may be interpreted as insensitive on another.

Avoid any sort of practical joke that might embarrass or humiliate a coworker or colleague. You may find yourself working with that colleague for years, and for that reason alone, you should avoid doing or saying anything that might result in him or her looking silly or less than professional.

Bathroom humor in any form does not belong in the office.

96. Manage wet weather

Inclement weather brings additional challenges to students and new professionals, who may need to tote umbrellas or wear snow boots into the office.

Carry appropriate-sized umbrellas to the office, and reserve golf umbrellas for the back nine. Before opening an umbrella, look around to ensure you won't poke a colleague or coworker.

When walking down the street with an umbrella, be cognizant of the people around you. To avoid crashing umbrellas, look for opportunities to carry yours higher or lower.

When entering an office building, immediately close any dripping umbrella that you have carried. Store it in a designated storage area. If the office has not designated a place for wet umbrellas, consider resting yours in your personal office trash bin until it dries. Then fold it closed and tuck it away.

Be aware that snow boots can track salt and grime throughout an office. If you must enter an office building in snow boots, change into office-appropriate shoes as soon as possible. Find a place to store your boots where residual snow and ice can melt without creating a mess on an office floor.

97. Bathroom etiquette

Several years ago, after I facilitated an etiquette dinner on a leading university campus, a group of five male law students approached and said two words: urinal etiquette. "You're going to have to help me out," I replied. "I don't have a lot of experience with this. What's the real issue?" One of the young men responded: "What are you supposed to do when you head to the bathroom, someone follows you in, and while the two of you are standing at the urinals, the other guy starts talking business?"

Here's what I told the group: if the other person is a peer, it seems to me you should be able say, "Hey, let's talk about this later. Why don't I stop by your office in 10 minutes or so."

If the other person is your boss or supervisor, you need to listen and respond. Keep your response as polite and succinct as possible… and keep your eyes trained straight ahead.

As to the ladies restroom, I've lost count of the number of women who complain about coworkers who use the restroom as their personal phone booth. If and when you need to make a private phone call, please find some other location to talk. Reserve restrooms for necessary bodily functions, brushing teeth, checking makeup, and combing hair.

98. Address someone's body odor

Before you complain about someone's body odor, be aware that any odor you detect may be the result of some underlying medical condition. As such, you should react to it with the same tolerance that you would show to any other special need.

If you have both a professional and a personal relationship with a person who has body odor, consider a private talk away from the office. You might say, "This is very difficult for me to say, but if the shoe were on the other foot, I'd want you to say something to me." Explain the situation and offer solutions, keeping close tabs on the person's emotional reaction.

If you feel uncomfortable having this conversation, quietly and discretely take the issue to Human Resources.

In the meantime, be sensitive about your own scent— good or bad. Use perfume or other fragrances sparingly. Every day you attend work, take a bath and use deodorant or an antiperspirant.

99. Respond to offensive remarks

Inevitably someone will say something that you find offensive. How you respond will say a great deal about you and the good manners you've developed.

Please don't reply in kind. Doing so will only diminish the good standing you've worked so hard to develop. When someone else says something foolish, don't be foolish in response.

In some cases, especially where the statement is thoughtless and meaningless, you may be able to say simply, "I respectfully disagree," and walk away. That will be the end of it.

However, when a statement genuinely offends you, make time for a quick private conversation. Referring to the exact phrasing that you found offensive—please, do not paraphrase—repeat what the person said and describe how it affected you. Keep your emotions in check. Don't question the speaker's intent or motive. And don't expect an apology. Make your case professionally and then move on.

100. Act with kindness

Every student and new professional has loads to learn when entering the world of work. Having a fundamental understanding of business etiquette certainly helps. By now I hope you understand that etiquette involves so much more than knowing when to lift a particular piece of silverware, how to execute a perfect handshake, or what to say when you draft a genuine thank-you note.

Truth be told, you can forget every other word that appears in this book as long as you remember these three: *act with kindness*. This truly is what good manners and business etiquette are all about.

As you start or relaunch your career, focus on becoming your best self. Always treat others with respect. Look for opportunities to act in thoughtful and caring ways. Build others up, and avoid tearing others down.

Understand that very little in the world of work is a zero-sum game. Look for opportunities to develop win-win solutions.

Keep in mind what Warren Buffet once said: "It takes twenty years to build a reputation and five minutes to ruin it. If you think about that, you'll do things differently."

Now go build your best reputation ever!

About the Author

A graduate of the University of Missouri and George Washington University Law School, Mary Crane lobbied in Washington, DC, for nearly ten years before pursuing her lifelong interests in food and wine. She enrolled in the Culinary Institute of America and, upon graduation, worked at the White House as an assistant chef. During this time, Crane discovered the important relationships between food, wine, and business. Her desire to share this unique knowledge yielded Mary Crane & Associates.

Today, Mary Crane travels North America delivering high-impact, high-energy programs to Fortune 500 companies, leading law firms, nonprofits and colleges and universities. She helps students, interns, and new hires successfully make the critically important transition from school to work.

Mary Crane has been featured on *60 Minutes, Fox Business News,* and *ABC Radio.* She has been quoted extensively in a variety of print and electronic media, including *The New York Times, The Wall Street Journal,* Forbes.com, Fortune.com, and CNN.com.

If you liked this book,
check out additional titles for new professionals in
Mary Crane's 100 Things You Need to Know series.

All are available on
at www.marycrane.com.

Made in the USA
San Bernardino, CA
08 February 2020